Some book reviews

"I found your style of writing very personal and easy to read (I get very bored reading long words). I also found the writings of clients very interesting and "real" and could relate to many of the feelings they talked of through my own experiences of parenting and working with other parents.

I will definitely be recommending your book to others. In fact I already have a list of those who I think will benefit although in an ideal world I would probably put it on an essentials list so every parent to be had to read it before the baby was born."
Penny Lazell RGN RHV, Health Visitor 4 U

"I love your whole concept of 'energetic connection' and I really like the way you make it so practical and down to earth because it is a little outside what some parents' experience and it is a great way to introduce them to it. It's a great introduction and it works really well.

I know the idea of connection runs through the whole book and it is a powerful message. It's really easy to dip into and every chapter gives me great ideas to help me be the Mum I want to be. It's also great and inspired that all parents can get ongoing support through the community website."
Lorraine Thomas, Chief Executive, The Parent Coaching Academy, Author, 'The 7-Day Parent Coach', 'Get A Life' and 'The Mummy Coach'

GW00587128

"A well thought and well written book involving every aspect of parenting starting from problem solving strategy to celebrating each step. A unique book with fun and entertaining exercises for kids. I really like the idea of a Happy Book for younger kids where the Author has adapted the 'Power of thought' and 'Power of Positive Affirmations' concepts which I believe works very well with the kids.

By adapting the techniques mentioned in this book will not just change an individual but the whole family. Parents today are under pressure to be perfect parents but this book allows a parent to enjoy the journey of parenting in a positive way.

A very inspiring quote that is dear to my heart... "To be in your children's memories tomorrow, you have to be in their lives today." - Barbara Johnson"

Seema Thobhani, Author of a series of 6 positive books for children and a Child Well-Being Consultant, Kidz4Mation Ltd

"This is not a typical parenting book; the focus is not on fixing but on maximizing potential! In this inspirational book Alan Wilson brings to life many wonderful, key concepts. This book will teach you how to empower you (as a parent) and your wonderful off spring!

I'm also delighted to inform, this book is congruent; it really does what it says on the tin!

"When you are at your most resourceful and set the intention to connect with someone who is equally receptive, you will open up a whole new world of connections and possibilities!!! This is magic in action."

This book focuses on the concept of 'energetic connections'. This is truly an eye opener. This book highlights the joys of being deeply connected with yourself and your children and provides you with resources to support you to unlock your parenting potential to maximise your parenting successes. Alan's writing allows you to experience his wonderful sensitivity and this goes a long way to help you to support the real needs of your children and young people."

Vivien Sabel UKCP. MBACP. ScPTI. MNCP, Writer, Researcher, Infant Body Language Expert, Parenting Expert, Psychotherapist & Mother

"The book contains photocopiable pages where parents can make note of their goals, aspirations and priorities. I loved the "Wheel of Life" which allows us to look at eight areas of life that are most important, and find ways to enhance these areas and coming up with one thing that could improve them right now. We can make SMART goals (specific, measurable, achievable, realistic and timed).

When we implement these exercises and start to see improvements in our own life, the positivity impacts on the whole family. We can learn to listen to our children, make them feel special and valued and help them to achieve their potential giving support, respect and appreciation. We are encouraged to celebrate our successes and share our achievements as a family."

Wendy, Inside the Wendy House

"It is unusual in that it does not simply tell you 'what to do' but gives you a series of personal development exercises showing you how to be happy and comfortable yourself, making a better parent and advising how to be a 'Parent Champion' to your family, perhaps easing the sometimes stressful road of raising children. It also offers free ongoing support within a community of like-minded parents."
Bloggomy

Some reviews of the approach

"Alan provides an insightful and accessible approach to helping families. Boldly encouraging parents to consider their energy and intuition, he taps into knowledge about how the human brain operates and reminds us that our outlook towards ourselves and others influences our communication – and the communication that we receive back. You can really hear his enthusiasm and having met Alan, I am not surprised to hear about the positive difference his courses are making."
Rachel Bamber, Brighter Thinking & Head of Assessments, Lead Trainer, NeuroLeadership Group. Rachel is 1 of the first 6 people in the world to achieve a Post-Graduate Certificate in the Neuro-science of Leadership, currently studying for the Master's

"Coaching is the practical tool to deliver strengths based 'Recovery Model' type interventions with families and individuals. I

am in support of using this approach to families both because of it's effectiveness and it's congruence with a person centred approach. From a more systemic perspective because it develops transferable skills it does have the potential for a viral impact. The DofH last year agreed with our proposal to use the Recovery Model to bring about coordinated multi agency direct practice with users of the new multi million pound centres for disabled children opening in Swale, Thanet and Ashford in April."
Graham Smith, East Kent Area Manager for Disabled Children's Services, Kent County Council

"Incorporating the concepts and using the tools in this book will magically transform your outlook on parenting and relationships."
Dr Rani Bora, MB BS, MRCPsych Psychiatrist, Life Coach and EFT practitioner

"One of the parents on the course (now Parent Champion level 2) asked me what she can do next and I advised her that any 'parenting' programme would in fact be a step backwards. I think there's real value to this programme and why shouldn't everyone access it? There's a definite gap to be filled, families that have had counselling or need a way to move on, especially with self esteem issues and also taking control of their lives – it's a perfect fit."
Mrs Anita Smith, Children and Families Coordinator, Bligh Children's Centre

"Awareness of the power of how deeper listening can transform relationships has helped me to engage more effectively with my students and they with each other; it forms the foundations of

powerful communication skills and builds self esteem."
Georgina Saralis, Deputy Head, SEN School

"Since starting on the course (now Parent Champion level 2), Mrs D has become more confident in her parenting of her children. She is more assertive in setting boundaries and can maintain those. Her confidence will hopefully allow her to make the right choices for her and her family even though they may not be easy ones. The social worker Tatjana Ramshaw has noticed a great difference."
Ms Caroline Lindesay, Senior Practitioner, Chatham Integrated Services Team

"To empower and respect anyone, never mind just your children, you have to first empower and respect yourself - and this book does a great job of teaching you how"
Martin Goodyer, MBPsS MAC, Business, Corporate & Executive Coaching

"I know that several parents attended the Parent Champion Programme over the last eight weeks and the teachers have been reporting back to me about the changes they have seen in the parents' relationships with the children and indeed the children themselves. The outcome has been very positive.

I can see the impact your programme is having and feel it is providing a vital service for parents. It is apparent that life is faster paced, often resulting in more stress for some families. The relationship that teachers have with parents has evolved with parents being more open, wanting to share their problems and seeking sources of advice. Parenting has always been a difficult job, never more so than now and so programmes such as yours are greatly needed to positively empower families.

Keep up the good work!."
Miss T J Gobell, Headteacher, Bligh Infant School

"Alan seems to really have a knack for inspiring single mums with confidence and getting things to look up for them and their kids"
Mark Reckless MP

I ~~don't~~ know you ~~anymore~~

7 steps to reconnect with your teenager

by **ALAN WILSON**
Develop Your Child CIC

Printed in the UK by Lightning Source UK Ltd
ISBN 978-0-9551130-5-5

I don't know you anymore

7 steps to reconnect with your teenager

by **ALAN WILSON**
Develop Your Child CIC

Contents

Preface

I believe that children are our future
Teach them well and let them lead the way
Show them all the beauty they possess inside
Give them a sense of pride to make it easier
Let the children's laughter remind us how we used to be
Everybody's searching for a hero
People need someone to look up to
I never found anyone who fulfilled my need
A lonely place to be and so I learned to depend on me
I decided long ago never to walk in anyone's shadow
If I fail, if I succeed at least I'll live as I believe
No matter what they take from me, they can't take away my dignity
Because the greatest love of all was happening to me
I found the greatest love of all inside of me
The greatest love of all is easy to achieve
Learning to love yourself is the greatest love of all
From the 'Greatest love of all' written by Michael Masser and Linda Creed

For me, these are the most beautiful words in the world. I love this song because it captures so many aspects of parenting and personal empowerment: the very essence of children, the importance of their own identity, their independence, the value of a role model and how much children can teach us if we allow them to!

Remember - if you keep doing what you've always done, you'll keep getting what you've always got.

I ~~DON'T~~ KNOW YOU ~~ANY~~MORE

Foreword

by Sir John Whitmore PhD

I love this book; I love Alan's style of using separate, clear and important sentences to make a large number of key points. It is a book that one can pick up for a short time while travelling and extract real thought provoking ideas and value. It really works for me and I expect it will for many others too. Alan challenges parents who are so obsessed with controlling their children and not allowing, let alone encouraging, them to be themselves. Who else can they be, may I ask? I am so delighted that he recognises the value of learner centred communication advocated by Carl Rogers, which is so apposite for children's education and development. Rogers was a great pioneer of human skills whose key work is still not fully appreciated or adopted. I was fortunate enough to know him and attend person-centred workshops with him at Esalen Institute in California in the 1970s.

We want our children to be self-responsible of course, but telling them to be often has the opposite effect. Offer them a choice and they will welcome the freedom that choices offer. A child soon discovers that all choices have consequences and by experiencing those consequences, they quickly learn how to make better choices. The act of making a choice gives instant self-responsibility, and the child continues to become a more skilful choice maker.

This massive benefit applies to all those things that may cause children lifelong difficulties if they make bad choices, such as: drugs, alcohol, food, anger, envy, exercise, fear, knives, sex, health, violence, people, and more. None of these are intrinsically bad but the consequences of bad choices in dealing with any of them may well be. Children begin to believe in themselves and feel better about themselves as they make good choices. I cannot emphasise more the importance of this. Alan never lets this slip from the readers mind.

My ex-wife created and runs an award winning teenage pregnancy programme for schools, one of the most effective in the country, which are based on these principles and I am an advisor for driver education which focuses on young male drivers who have far more fatalities than other age or sex sectors throughout Europe because of their inability to make sensible choices. This issue of encouraging choice making, in my mind is the single and most important psychologically healthy and life giving principle that is missing from education and parenting. This must change and I hope the relevant authorities read this book and wake up to it.

The structure of this book is excellent for its purpose of reaching all kinds of parents easily and in very direct simple language. At the beginning Alan lays out the purpose and intent of the book and then goes on to express very clearly his philosophy and thinking behind it. It has qualities, readability and clarity that is rare in many academic books about parenting and education. Many of Alan's statements are memorable and quotable, and at the start of each chapter is an entirely relevant quote from a well-known figure.

In the book Alan challenges 'conventional' thinking in how to communicate and connect with your children. It is a natural process, which as he says creates the opportunity for the parent to parent naturally. Alan has been pioneering this approach, which has shown remarkable results. Parents can choose to be happy, congruent and trust their instincts; this is an innate process, which needs to be developed. I was fortunate enough to witness him in action and I must say I was astounded at the effect on his coachee - I thought it was brilliant.

Alan offers a large number of exercises that have great value when undertaken fully. They are for action not just reading and passing over, as people are often tempted to do. He also advises people to photocopy the exercise pages for their use so the book remains unmarked, but he suggests that several copies are made so the exercises can be done several times over the passage of time, six months or even a year or two. A great idea is to involve the whole family. Alan also includes in most chapters pieces written by people after attending one of his courses. Alan is also unafraid to reveal some of his own struggles in life, which makes the reader see him as human like all of us, and not infallible as some writers pretend.

I could not recommend a book or an approach to education in these difficult times more strongly than I feel about this one. Alan has a passion, like my own, to change education to allow children to believe in themselves. This will have huge impact and create a more self-responsible society; I think we all want that! Whilst it is primarily intended for teachers and parents, I believe that many more of us can benefit from reading it and doing the exercises.

Try it and then tell others about it.

"Do your children listen to you?"
"Not very well or often"
"How well or often do you really listen to your children?"

Acknowledgements

To the three most important people in my life, my children Toby, Holly and Cassy, for all they have taught me and continue to do so.

Also Emma Anderson, Claire Ashby, John Bayford, Phil Browne, Peter Burke, Mike and Anne Bushell, Vee Cadby, Richard Carey, Sonya Chowdhury, Alan Chuck, Anca Ciobanu, Andrei Ciursa, Barry Clout, Toni Clarke, Martha Collins, Kirsty Cruttenden, Hanife Dacosta, Della Dingwall, Christine Doorbar, Richard Earp, Dorothy Eckes, Thrity Engineer, Shinina Fernandez, Nic Fiddaman, Sandra Garrod, Diane Graham, Santari Green, Soleira Green, Tina Gobell, Andy and Sue Gower, Karen Halliday, Derek Handy, Fiona Harrold, Diana Haskins, Steve Hatt, Lynne Healy, Mark Holmes, Geraldine Hurstfield, John Hyatt, Terry Ingham, Paula Jago, Ernie and Gill Jones, Noelyne Jones, Stuart Kerslake, LaJeanne Kline, Marci Lebowitz, Ian Lewis, Debra Littleboy, Ian Longstaff, Michael Low, Jane MacAllister Dukes, Kerry McMorris, Dr Roger Mills, Judith Morgan, Juliet Platt, Alan Povey, Dick and Linda Reynolds, Sandra Rounthwaite, Anthony Sands, Georgina Saralis, Debbie Simpson, Andrew Smith, Janet Swift, David and Rosalind Taylor, Graham Taylor, Jo Trice, John Turner, Linda Turner, Ann Waters, Lisa Waters, Mary Whelan, Susan Wilson, Clare Whiston, Gemma White, John and Irene Whiting, Sir John Whitmore, Sarah Wilkins, Georgina Woudstra and Vivienne Wrelton, Ady Young who have all contributed in some way to my personal growth and the value of this book.

Preamble

Welcome to my world of infinite possibilities - this book is going to change you and the way you parent forever.

You know how a Mum instinctively knows, when she is relaxed, what her baby wants - I believe that depth of connection is always available to us, and not just to Mums.

This is not a typical parenting book or a typical self-help book. Generally a parenting book is focused on 'fixing' your child, this book helps you see your children from a different perspective.

More than a self-help book, it comes with a series of personal development exercises. You will not only be a better parent you will also get your life back.

The bottom line is for you to be happy and comfortable in yourself and when you are - you will parent naturally.

Have you noticed how when you're happy everything is a breeze and you sail through any challenge? By becoming your most powerful self, you will have a deeper connection with your children and add magic to your family.

This book won't be looking at teenage behaviour or its causes. We will show how to make changes in yourself, which dramatically change your relationship with your teen. And you will have the tools and techniques to unleash their potential.

We are breaking the mould in three critical areas:

1. We recognise children are sensitive to parents' emotional state and take responsibility for it – happy parents equals happy children.

2. We provide a unique personal development approach to create self-awareness, change and sustainability in you first and then your children.

3. Parents can parent naturally and create empowered and resilient families, whose influence overflows into their community, helping to create a more positive society.

How do I know this is possible? I've been there and done it. After bankruptcy, divorce and a nervous breakdown all within 12 months, I was far from the ideal parent. I recognised that, as I became more positive and personally empowered, my relationship with my children changed dramatically, as did their view of themselves and relationship with each other. This book is the distillation of all the great things I learnt on my journey from that place.

Alan Wilson – Family Coach

Introduction

If I had my child to raise over again

'If I had my child to raise over again,
I'd finger paint more, and point the finger less.
I'd do less correcting, and more connecting.
I'd take my eyes off my watch, and watch with my eyes.
I would care to know less, and know to care more.
I'd take more hikes and fly more kites.
I'd stop playing serious, and seriously play.
I'd run through more fields, and gaze at more stars.
I'd do more hugging, and less tugging.
I would be firm less often, and affirm much more.
I'd build self-esteem first, and the house later.
I'd teach less about the love of power,
And more about the power of love.'
Diane Loomans

This book is about helping you to reconnect with your children at a deeper level. Once you have achieved this, you will be connecting with them in a whole new way and opening a whole new world full of possibilities for both of you.

The word 'empower' tends to be overused but I make no excuses for adopting it because it captures the essence of our work - to create personal empowerment in parents. The Cambridge International Dictionary of English definition says 'something that is empowering makes you more confident and makes you feel that you are in control of your life'.

My role is to help you identify that 'something' so you can create the respectful and resilient family relationships you desire.

Children are our future and we, as parents have the most challenging job in the world. Children don't come with a manual and there are no 'one size fits all' solutions. The decline of the extended family, coupled with the influence of persuasive advertising, online challenges and a 'have it now' mentality, means that successful parenting has become increasingly difficult. That's without all the pressure we put on ourselves to be the perfect parent.

The area of emotions is critical. How often are we beating ourselves up because we are falling short of our own expectations of ourselves? But I say to parents "what did you learn about 'emotional literacy' at school?" so lets be gentle with ourselves and have more fun!

There is a great deal of interest and media attention on how we communicate with our children. What's missing is the understanding that parents are doing the best they can with what they know and that communication is much more than just talking and listening.

In my work with parents, I'm regularly asked "how can I get little Charlie to listen to me?" If I replied, "well, have you listened to him?" in some cases I might well have risked physical injury! By 'listening' I don't mean just to the words that a child says; I mean what lies behind the words - i.e. deep listening - what is that wonderful small person trying to communicate to you?

I coined the phrase 'energetic listening/connection' as a generic phrase, it could also be known as instincts, intuition, gut feeling, sensing, love etc. Some children call it magic! It's a very powerful process that needs a little guidance in how to become aware of it, although it's innate in all of us and is happening all the time. It allows a deeper connection with the person you are communicating with. Mastering this process/art is the foundation of fulfilling relationships and it works with children, teens and adults.

Many parents have low self-esteem and little time for themselves. They find it very difficult, if not impossible, to communicate effectively with their children. Parents can choose to feel better about themselves and try new tools and techniques to enable them to take a new approach to life.

Sometimes that choice isn't always clear or easy to take because they may feel locked into a cycle of reactive behaviours, and to step out of their comfort zone is a challenge too far. I can only say if you don't change something in your life, you will keep getting what you've always got. Freedom can be achieved by increasing your personal empowerment. And that's exactly what this book is about.

When a parent connects with a child or teen in this way, their whole life and family relationships change! They parent naturally.

When parents show respect for what their child has to say and allow them to experience, even in a small way, their own independence, the changes are immense - and it spreads throughout the whole family.

I've seen this with almost every parent I've worked with as a Family Coach and Parenting Tutor. There is a case study at the end of each Chapter to give you some real life examples of how some parents and carers have transformed their families and the tools and techniques they used.

These case studies are taken from groups of parents who've

attended courses and an independent evaluation is available on the www.developyourchild.co.uk website. During a course there are time limitations so we are usually only able to cover a fraction of the content of this book.

Most parents are run ragged, going round in circles in an attempt to keep everything together at all costs – mostly to themselves. Once I get them to hear me - and that's not easy – I teach them to look at themselves as individuals and to work towards their own personal empowerment. This has to be felt in the body, the mind and the heart before it really kicks in. When parents discover this for themselves, they feel empowered, then everything changes in the way they want it to.

I come from a life coaching background – that is taking you from where you are now to where you want to be. Life coaching and associated techniques create self-empowerment. An empowered parent is a congruent parent more open to change. Coaches are non-judgmental; we value our clients' gifts and support them to recognise these gifts and to move forward in their lives.

I've worked directly and indirectly with thousands of parents and carers to create this unique personal development approach, over the last 11 years, to build family resilience and self-responsibility

Any personal development work needs to begin with a sound foundation in self-esteem/confidence and that is always my starting point. The most common complaint I hear from children and young people is that their parents don't listen to them, value them or respect them.

My belief is that we are all born wonderful, resourceful, creative and full of potential - and then life kicks in! I see my role as a facilitator helping reconnect both children and parents with their innate abilities and then engaging them together.

I also believe that children these days are more right-brained and creative. This leads to disaffection in school; the National Curriculum is largely biased towards academia, left-brain functionality. Through no fault of their own, teachers have become starved of opportunities to develop the inter-action with children, which attracted them into the profession in the first place.

I read some research recently that showed children required acknowledgement, empathy and acceptance with and from their peer group and that that is more important to them than achieving academic success.

I don't know if you've heard of the Generation Y or Millennial Generation thought to be born from the early 1980s to the early 2000s. These young people are said to be hypersensitive, feel their way through life and sense a lack of authenticity and will switch off. This is providing challenges for society, business and education.

I personally feel that the most important aspect of an education is to explore the innate gifts and abilities an individual has and to help them identify their passion. There are so many young people diagnosed with 'Special Education Needs' who are actually very creative and skilled but are challenged in an academic setting.

We are working to introduce our unique approach into mainstream education where the teachers, pupils and parents are working together to change the culture of the learning environment.

It won't be long now before the education system explodes or implodes!

The Government is putting more and more pressure on parents to take responsibility for their children's behaviour - truancy, ASBOs, bullying etc, whilst providing woefully inadequate support.

There is no support for parents of teenagers, when communication can start to breakdown (does 'teenage' start at 7 years old these days?). This is the critical time when parents and children start to go their separate ways. The tragedy is that the children tend to rely on their peers and their peers cannot help them emotionally, with life experiences or wisdom.

There is a huge gap in emotional literacy and that is the root cause of so much misunderstanding and conflict.

Parents, particularly those under pressure, need comprehensive and integrated support that they can access without feeling stigmatised. It doesn't exist and the increase in family breakdown has further wide-ranging, detrimental effects on children.

It doesn't matter whether or not you have the same views as I have; I just want you to know where I'm coming from in the hope that it will give you some more options.

How you feel about yourself is the single most important awareness you can take away from this book. Together we will look at the tools and techniques I have found to be very effective and simple to use.

There are a number of exercises throughout the book, so you may want to photocopy the pages or transfer the details to a separate notebook or journal. By keeping the book pristine others can do the exercises. And you can redo them after 6 months or so to see your progress. A great idea is to include your children and family in these exercises.

Our children are facing unprecedented rates of change and we are trying to prepare them for jobs that don't yet exist, using technologies that haven't been invented in order to solve problems we don't yet know about.

There has never been a more important time to create personal empowerment in children and young people.

Over the last 50 years, the relentless pace of change has brought with it intolerable social and financial pressures. For many of us, feelings and emotions have been dulled down until we have, almost literally, disconnected from our bodies.

As a result, our behaviour has become little more than a series of, usually inappropriate, reactions to our experiences, which leave us unable to trust our own instincts/intuition/gut feeling.

Adults who take the time to understand and develop themselves are better able to trust this vital power. They can raise their children to be aware of its importance – and teach them how to use it. We must empower our children to develop this skill because they will be responsible for the world's future.

The book is in three parts to take you from where you are to where you want to go.

Part 1 – It starts with you. We need to get you in a place where you can tap into your most resourceful. As you are starting to make these changes those around you will have noticed them and it's likely you will be tested. That's OK and normal because the vast majority of people are not comfortable with change, just like you before you started!

Part 2 – When they are ready. As you become more familiar and comfortable with these tools and techniques you will no doubt want to give your children the benefit of them. This part of the book is for when they are ready. The most important step is not to force this on them, just carry on being your powerful self and exceptional role model. Soon they will recognise the value in wanting to change and will ask when they are ready – fantastic!

And **Part 3 – Additional resources.** In this section there are some additional tools and techniques, which you may find useful if they are appropriate for you.

We will touch on many aspects and concepts that you may want to explore further. If you need further guidance, please contact me info@everyfamilymatters.org.uk and I will do all I can to help.

It's time to brace yourself for the ride of your life and create the life you deserve!

NB.   This book is written for you. However, when you want to apply these tools and techniques to others you may need to adapt some of your questions and exercises to suit that persons stage of development. As a parent of a teen this can be a challenge as they have been subjected to all sorts of influences outside the home. This has probably pushed them further from you, so the changes you are making will be tested and will call for you to be resolute in your determination to change.

But have faith and trust yourself, every parent I know who has been determined has been successful. We've had loads of parents telling us things like "I don't know what your doing Mum but don't stop" or "You're so much calmer now and I love you again" and "You've changed so much Mum, how did you do it?"

Also if you want a reminder – ask yourself – were you happy going round in the same circles day after day after day?

For the sake of expediency 'child' includes adolescence, teenagers and young people.

Case Study Mrs KA

"I'm going to hold my hand up and be totally honest: when I embarked on the Parent Champion course, I wondered, deep down, whether this course was really going to be worth the time commitment - eight weeks of two hour sessions - required. I wasn't really sure what to expect; indeed it all sounded a little nebulous. So I approached the course without the degree of enthusiasm it deserved from me!

After two sessions, something clicked, and I could sense subtle changes in the way I thought about many things, not simply my family life. Interestingly, the course started just as we were going through some particularly difficult issues with my oldest daughter (it's funny how these 'coincidences' occur, isn't it?!) and I am convinced that the turn-around we have seen in her is in large part due to the - very small but very significant - changes brought about by the Parent Champion course.

I was at a very low ebb right at the beginning, wondering how on earth we would manage to help our daughter. The support provided not only by the course guidance, but also by the other parents in our group, were both key to me being able to embark on a new approach. It is still hard work staying on track, and it is all too easy to slip into old habits, but it is possible - and life-changing.

My approach to the problems we were having at the time was to keep open the lines of communication with our teenage daughter. I had seen too many families experience difficulties through poor or no communication, and I was determined that this would not happen to us. However, subtle changes in me led me to 'know' intuitively and instinctively that I needed to be clearer in my approach to my daughter - even if she didn't like what I had to say - rather than fudge issues as I had been doing. In addition to this, I was able to put responsibility for her actions back 'in her court', rather than feel responsible myself for every misdemeanour that occurred. But at the same time, I was able to listen - deeply listen on a totally different level to before - to what she had to say. We are on a different track now, a more positive one, which feels much better, and I feel much more optimistic about the choices she is making, as does she.

It would take a chapter in a book to explain the many and different changes I have observed; taken individually, they seem tiny, but it is the sum total of their combination, and the profound effect they have had, that is huge.

Some aspects were much easier to harness than I had thought they would be, for example, the encouragement to be aware of making judgemental comments. 'Letting judgement go' was considerably easier than I had expected – it was almost a relief, making me feel freer in spirit!

Our group consisted mainly of mums – with one long-suffering dad – and it was interesting how every single person professed to feelings of guilt at taking time out for themselves. It's not easy choosing to do something that is all about you, when you have spent so many years thinking and planning with everyone else's interests in mind. With practice, it is achievable, and it is truly uplifting to spend time doing something you really enjoy – which of course has an effect on your family, as you are in a better 'place' when you have taken time out. Indeed, they like this 'different person' who miraculously emerges at home!

I feel more light-hearted, as though a burden has been lifted from my shoulders. I don't worry as much as I used to, particularly about things I cannot possibly affect – and this was a real problem for me as I used to take on the world's heavy load, knowing, and feeling very sad in this knowledge, that I could only touch a micro-fraction of it. I am more able to accept the limits of what I can do. (Another concept I gained from the course – don't be so hard on yourself all the time!)

And I have been reminded by the course that our thoughts cause our actions. Indeed, with the latter point in mind, I recall a beautiful and very true quotation that says: 'Energy follows thought and thought attracts its own kind' – something to bear in mind on those days when I am not naturally inclined to be truly, energetically positive in my thoughts. Each one of us can affect the world around us by subtle shifts in what we think and do.

All these – and many more — aspects need working on, as there are so many old habits that have built up over the years. But there is no doubt that, by following this path, you won't simply be enhancing your qualities as a parent, but also as a person. By so doing, there are no limits to what you can achieve."
Mrs KA

"PS: I understand that the course is for parents and children. Perhaps I have missed something, but are teachers usually included within the course framework? Are there Teacher Champion courses? At our school, some teachers have been given the opportunity of being involved within the course, but this is clearly not possible for all during school hours. The teachers' frame of mind and their energy profoundly affect the school atmosphere,

I DON'T KNOW YOU ANYMORE

and therefore the progress of the students, so it seems to me that it is crucial that they are as involved in this life-changing mindset as us parents are."

CHAPTER 1

Why this book?

Priorities

A hundred years from now it will not matter what my bank account was, the sort of house I lived in, or the kind of car I drove, but the world may be different because I was important in the life of a child...
Forest Witcraft

Perhaps I should start by telling you about how my beliefs and life events combined to put me where I am today. See also Appendix IV - Why I'm the luckiest Dad in the World.

1. I've always felt that school didn't properly prepare children for life. I couldn't be specific then - but I can now. Today's curriculum has very little, if any, emphasis on building self-esteem, emotional literacy or life skills.

2. I've always been inquisitive about what makes people tick. I'm always saying 'penny for your thoughts' and I was the pain at parties asking 'why?'. Not the best question in a life coaching context as it puts people on the defensive and you're not going to learn very much from their response – except how to duck!

3. In my previous life of advertising and marketing, I was always challenging clients and supporting them to come up with a different or unique solution. I was quite happy even if that strategy was successful even if that solution meant they would not be spending their promotional budget with me.

4. I was lucky enough to get a second chance with my parenting role, having a daughter later in life. I realised I wanted to "do it differently" this time around.

5. I found the power of life coaching and was swept off my feet with the positive, future-orientated approach that encouraged you to accept the past and, instead, looked at where you wanted to be and inspired you to create a strategy to get there.

6. At the same time I found my passion – to holistically develop children. I started writing programmes for children of all ages to create a sound foundation of self-esteem and confidence.

7. I found, all too often, that any child with a problem had a parent or carer with a bigger problem - usually emotional.

8. And I wanted to build on the work since my first book "Listen to your children... and they will listen to you".

All of these things have come together to enable me to help create respectful and fulfilling family relationships for others and myself. I achieved this by using my experience of life, life coaching and related techniques, and the laws of the Universe to empower children and the people who influence them. I've been on this particular path for the last eleven years and seen huge transformations in families, so I wanted to share this with you.

I believe every child has limitless potential. It starts as a spark, which needs to be identified, protected, nurtured, developed and respected. This spark must grow into a strong flame to survive the school system, parents under pressure and the influence of some peers.

Together, we will fan the flames of self-esteem and confidence to explode the potential of the world's children.

My vision now is to take this approach into schools and work with the teachers, support staff, pupils and parents to create a whole school ethos of empowerment around young people, to change the culture of the learning environment.

Children don't come with a manual. If they did, it would need to be online – because it changes every day/minute. But children are our future and we, as parents, have what is the most challenging and most fulfilling job in the world and we learn as we go. We are all a work in progress.

Other than drawing on our own childhood memories and experiences, there is little preparation for parenting. Added to that are the pressures from society and even more stressful, all those pressures we put on ourselves.

With so much information for parents these days, it's easy to become confused and not really know where to go or who to trust.

It's also possible that our memories of how we were raised are not those we want to replicate with our own children.

Dr Tanya Byron a leading clinical psychologist, who used to produce 'The House of Tiny Tearaways' and various parenting programmes said "I'm not doing any more parenting programmes as a clinician at all. I think it's important that parents find their own way with their children that advice is helpful, but you need to trust your own instincts. I do still do one day a week clinical work and I find a lot of parents come to me feeling completely disempowered, because there's a lot of advice and they don't know what to use."

I propose an approach that allows parents to trust their instincts and be able to parent naturally – that is what this book is all about.

Bringing up a child is not easy. However, as you already know, the difficulties are more than outweighed by the joy of watching your child grow, develop and thrive.

It is my desire that this approach will be one of the best things you will ever do for yourself and your child, and will be extremely fulfilling for you both.

There is a clear distinction between this approach and the range of 'parenting' programmes available.

This unique approach has evolved over 11 years and been co-created with 1,000's of children, young people, parents and professionals working in homes, schools and Children's Centres. The theoretical approach is a rich mixture of advanced coaching, emotional literacy, Neuroscience and the work of Perls, Kolb, Jung and Rogers.

Fritz Perls (1893-1970) developed Gestalt Therapy, which focused on raising self-awareness in order to distinguish between a person's true nature and the personality they have developed in order to adapt to their environment. By becoming aware of their true nature, a person can then identify ways to achieve what makes them happy.

David A. Kolb (1939) has developed a theory (experiential learning) on the ways in which adults more successfully learn. He believes that we learn best by having hands-on experience of whatever it is we are learning and by then reflecting on our experiences, which then leads to greater absorption of the subject matter.

Carl Jung (1875-1961) made a huge contribution to the way in which we view the nature of human development and existence. One of these contributions was the idea of the Collective Unconscious, which is the linking of all people in the deepest part of our minds.

Carl Rogers (1902-1987) developed the person-centred psychotherapy approach in which he believed that if a person was provided with a totally accepting, non-judgemental relationship they would then be able to resolve their difficulties and find ways to successfully restructure their lives.

What does that mean? It means although our approach is innovative, it is soundly based on proven theories and when it comes to your precious relationships - that is very important.

Using advanced coaching, emotional literacy and Neuroscience we empower parents to see themselves differently, make changes for themselves and their children, to change their whole family dynamic and parent naturally.

Relevant definitions

Coaching (from Wikipedia)

Coaching refers to the activity of a coach in developing the abilities of a coachee. Coaching tends to focus on an existing problem (from which to move away) or a specific outcome that the individual wishes to achieve (move towards). In both cases, the coach aims to stimulate the coachee to uncover innate knowledge so they can achieve a sustainable result. Coaches will normally check that the specific learning can be successfully re-applied by the coachee, to deal with other problems in the future.

The structure and methodologies of coaching are very numerous with one unifying feature, coaching approaches are predominantly facilitating in style; that is to say that the coach is mainly asking questions and challenging the coachee to learn from their own resources. The coaching process is underpinned by established trust in the coachee. Coaching is differentiated from therapeutic and counselling disciplines in that the problems and outcomes have contexts which are important in the present and with aims for the future - these do not have emotional aetiology, or baggage, from the past - in other words, the coachee has the resources they need to make reasoned progress at the time that they seek coaching.

Coaching is often confused with mentoring, the difference is that a mentor will give advice based on the mentees experience and a coach will ask a question that will facilitate the coachee to find the answer they have inside.

It's surprising how coaching has and is featuring in our everyday lives. For instance how Lionel Louge the speech therapist in the wonderful

"The Kings Speech" film, used coaching techniques, see Appendix I. Also how coaching is being used in mental health to help patients focus on their strengths and improve their lives in Appendix II.

Sir John Whitmore introduced coaching and leadership into major multinationals in the UK over 30 years ago, and today it's used in almost 90% of companies. Sir John is now the Chairman of our charity Every Family Matters.

Emotional literacy (from Wikipedia)

Emotional Literacy is a term that was used first by Steiner (1997) who says: Emotional Literacy is made up of 'the ability to understand your emotions, the ability to listen to others and empathise with their emotions, and the ability to express emotions productively. To be emotionally literate is to be able to handle emotions in a way that improves your personal power and improves the quality of life around you. Emotional literacy improves relationships, creates loving possibilities between people, makes co-operative work possible, and facilitates the feeling of community.

He breaks emotional literacy into 5 parts:

1. *Knowing your feelings.*
2. *Having a sense of empathy.*
3. *Learning to manage our emotions.*
4. *Repairing emotional damage.*
5. *Putting it all together: emotional interactivity.*

Having its roots in counselling, it is a social definition that has inter-actions between people at it's heart. According to Steiner emotional literacy is about understanding your feelings and those of others to facilitate relationships, including using dialogue and self-control to avoid negative arguments. The ability to be aware and read other people's feelings enables one to interact with them effectively so that powerful emotional situations can be handled in a skillful way. Steiner calls this 'emotional interactivity'.

Steiner's model of emotional literacy is therefore primarily about dealing constructively with the emotional difficulties we experience to build a sound future. He believes that personal power can be increased and relationships transformed. The emphasis is on the individual, and as such encourages one to look inward rather than to the social setting in which an individual operates.

Thank goodness emotional literacy is finding it's way more into the National Curriculum because it is such a critical knowledge to have. I particularly liked the quote from the film 'The Secret' where Dr John Hagelin PhD. A.B.M.A said "We are using at most 5% of the potential of the human mind, 100% of human potential is the result of proper education. So imagine a world where people are using their full mental and emotional potential. We could go anywhere, we could do anything, achieve anything."

Neuroscience (from Wikipedia)

Neuroscience is the scientific study of the nervous system. Tradition-ally, neuroscience has been seen as a branch of biology. However, it is currently an interdisciplinary science that collaborates with other fields such as psychology, mathematics, physics, chemistry, engineering, computer science, philosophy and medicine. The term neurobiology is usually used interchangeably with the term neuroscience, although the former refers specifically to the biology of the nervous system, whereas the latter refers to the entire science of the nervous system.

The scope of neuroscience has broadened to include different approaches used to study the molecular, cellular, developmental, structural, functional, evolutionary, computational and medical aspects of the nervous system. The techniques used by neuroscientists have also expanded enormously, from molecular and cellular studies of individual nerve cells to imaging of sensory and motor tasks in the brain. Recent theoretical advances in neuroscience have also been aided by the study of neural networks.

NB. These three definitions have been taken from Wikipedia for consistency and online there are additional links to other entries for further explanation.

Here's a very straightforward explanation from Daniel Goleman's 'Social Intelligence' "Neuroscience has discovered that our brain's very design makes it sociable, inexorably drawn into an intimate brain-to-brain linkup whenever we engage with another person. That neural bridge lets us affect the brain - and so the body - of everyone we interact with, just as they do us."

Science is justifying what I know to be true and seen in action.

We have to want a different result before we start any personal development work. It's not easy to step out of our comfort zone and it requires determination. Over and above this, we need an understanding of how our thoughts and feelings affect our behaviour. I've heard it said that "we are what we think" very profound and absolutely true. Once we become truly aware of this, we can start to develop our own empowerment and identify our passion.

This will help us to connect with our intuition, which is, consciously or – for most of us - subconsciously, the driving force in our lives. Many of you might recognise this as your 'gut feeling' or instincts. Generally, we ignore this in order to 'keep the peace' externally, at the expense of keeping our peace internally. I believe that, when we learn to trust our intuition/instincts we are self-empowered.

The earlier children learn these techniques, the more enriched and fulfilling their life will be. This belief underpins all my work and is underwritten by my coaching philosophy.

Today's children are incredibly sensitive to the emotions of people around them - rather like barometers are sensitive to changes in the weather. And, from their perspective, when they sense that you are stressed or unhappy, they feel responsible and want to make things better for you.

The causes of your stress or unhappiness may be nothing to do with them. But your children don't know that. You may be doing the best you can to shield them from what's going on, but they can feel your discomfort. When they ask you what's the matter and you say "nothing": because you want to protect them or don't have time to explain, they can sense you are not telling the truth and not being authentic or congruent.

You may be doing the best you can to protect your children. But they are confused by mixed messages. This can have a detrimental effect on their self-esteem and confidence. Because what they are feeling/sensing doesn't match what they're being told, they start to doubt themselves. If this goes on too long, they lose confidence in themselves and start to 'act up'. That's when parents can get frustrated and try, in vain, to control their behaviour.

Parents know when they are happy their children are happy but what very few know is that their children, being sensitive to a parents emotional state, also take responsibility for that emotional state. Children don't have the confidence or the communication and emotional abilities to express their concern, so they kick off in the only way they know how to get attention. That might be screaming, hitting out or storming out of the room shouting "you don't understand me" as they slam the door.

If you can accept you don't actually have control over your children's behaviour and the best you can do is influence them positively, then you are making progress. How you influence your children depends on the quality of the relationship you have and the way you behave.

Just how do they know what kind of mood you're in before you enter the room? This is where our unique personal development approach comes in.

Children feel they are not listened to, valued or respected. It's true too, that many adults feel the same about children – so it's our choice, as adults if we want to change things. Knowing how to develop a high-quality relationship maybe the most important skill in parenting.

Our children are facing unprecedented rates of change in technology, communication, population dynamics and culture. We are trying to prepare our children for jobs that don't yet exist, using technologies that haven't been invented in order to solve problems we don't yet know about. And as a society we can't even deal with the problems we have now.

Today's parents need new skills and I'm not talking about 'parenting skills', I'm talking about personal development skills.

You know how 'Supernanny' tells parents what to do and then leaves them for a while and comes back to chaos? Well, our approach is different. I believe you already innately know what's best for you; you just don't always trust yourself. We ask you, as parents, breakthrough questions so you can find the answers you already have inside. Then we ask you questions that will motivate and inspire you to create your own strategy to go forward.

These skills are behind our unique personal development techniques – you'll find more in this book.

Can you imagine what life your children will have when they become self-empowered? They will be able to discover gifts, abilities and passions neither you nor they, knew they had, and they will be able to reach their full potential. WOW!

What an awesome gift you are giving your children.

Children develop at different speeds, learn with different preferences and are influenced by many outside role models. This may present a further challenge but such challenges are part of being a parent. Using a personal development approach can involve and include your child in identifying their best way forward.

This approach is designed to contribute to your continued development of you as a parent - a parent whom your child values and holds in high esteem. It gives you some ideas to help you both, in partnership, to maximize your potential and live life to the full.

Case Study Mrs Z

"Before I started the course I was at my wits end with my life and my children. I had no relationship with my eldest daughter except shouting at one another. I felt a failure as a mother and the life and relationships I wanted was far away and I could not reach them. I had no idea how I could change things to get that life and those relationships I wanted desperately.

I always saw the worst in everything I did or was going to do. I dreaded every day whether or not to argue with my eldest or someone was going to tell me I was doing it all wrong. I was on a roller coaster that wouldn't stop! I needed help but didn't know where to go.

At her school I was introduced to the home school support worker who helped me tremendously. She asked me if I'd heard of the course and explained a bit about it and asked if I'd like to go on it. I agreed to go because it sounded like it could really help. I was so scared of what might happen and how people would look at me but I knew I needed to do it.

My first session was scary, I didn't know how to process what was going on. I was scared to go as I thought I was admitting that I had failed. But when I was there I realised there were other parents feeling the same as me and that I was a good person. I just needed a different approach to things.

I was sceptical on how the course would help me and my children but I kept an open mind. (Each week put the bit in place that the trainer spoke to us about and started seeing changes in myself.) I was calmer and more patient with my children and others. My mum started to see how I handled situations calmly and dealing with the children's problems in an efficient manner without stressing and shouting.

I now realised I was a very stressed person and my energetic core was very fuzzy to myself and when I connect more energetically I found things very difficult to cope with, but I now enjoy spending time with myself and my children. I share more problems with the people closest to me to find better solutions to my problem if I cannot find one. I know now that success in life can be big or small and mean more to me than anyone else. I praise my children more for their successes and have a better relationship with my eldest.

I also think about the consequences more and choose not to do things that have bad consequences. I allow my children to solve their own problems and find their own answers with a little guidance to help them grow into even better adults and parents.

Other people have noticed changes in me and asked how. I have told them about the course and how it's helped me and how grateful I am for everything it has shown me.

I got with my partner in October when I was low and relied on him a lot. Whilst doing this course he could see a change in me *and the children. He did not like this and put me down a lot. I did not argue with him instead I sat and thought about things and then spoke to him in a reasonable manner but he always made it about him. I think he didn't like me being stronger than him.*

I am going to keep practicing everything I have been shown as I know I have still got a long way to go before my life and relationships are the way I want them to be. The relationship with my children will keep growing and they are a lot happier and relaxed.

I know now good things happen if you believe they will. Positive energy not negative!!!! I will let my children make their own choices as I do not own them. They are our FUTURE!!

I would like to see myself go back to college to get qualifications I need to become an accountant, then get a job and see my children grow into loving and beautiful adults.

Thanks to the course for showing me a new and better way to look at life that works for me. I am a good person and deserve more and so do my children."
Mrs Z.

"PS Also during the course I moved house!!!"

CHAPTER 2

Getting in the mood

Success is not the key to happiness. Happiness is the key to success. If you love what you are doing, you will be successful.
Albert Schweitzer

The biggest challenge today is the pace of life and we are trying to do too much too quickly. Also there is a strong belief that we cannot change our lives, and this book addresses that belief. The other challenge is for you to value yourself enough to create some 'me' time and that is what this chapter covers.

As a parent you have lots of juggling to do but if you want to help develop your child you must be in the right frame of mind and take a fresh look at your life.

You may need to consider changing your current habits and look at creating new ones. After all, if you keep doing what you're doing, you'll just keep getting what you're getting now! Simply committing yourself to making one small improvement each day can make all the difference.

It can be as easy as that. In reality it is not always that easy because you've tried it before and keep going around in the same circles. If you are serious about wanting to make a change in your life and are ready to work at it, then let's start you on the path now. You will gain a great deal from this exercise including getting some clarity and a different sense of priorities in your life.

There are a number of worksheets in this chapter that you may want to copy so that you can use them in the future. I do these exercises every 6 months or so. It is incredible how much can change in that short space of time when you have a different focus and start to create momentum. Some people create a journal to capture the key learning points as they evolve.

Step 1

Preparation

Before you start each exercise, get into an energised and positive frame of mind to get yourself motivated. Think about what makes you feel good and do it for a while!

- take a brisk walk
- play some music loudly and sing along to it
- stand up and have a big stretch
- jump up and down ten times
- stand outside and take some deep breaths of fresh air
- think of something you enjoy and breathe deeply
- think about the best your life could be. Where are you? What are you doing? Who are you with? etc.

Step 2

Don't fall into the trap of just looking at what's wrong or what you feel you don't do well.

Start noticing and take time to reflect on what you do well! Go one step further and make a list to keep near you as a reminder. This can provide a great boost to your confidence and self-esteem, which really can help you to push through barriers and move you forward towards what you want.

So, are you ready to make a commitment to yourself and start creating a life that you love?

What I do well

Make a list of at least 6 things you 'do well' and more if you can. The more you do, the better you will feel and when you think you've completed the list make an effort to come up with one or two more. The ones that are locked away are the gems!

1. _____

2. _____

3. _____

4. _____

5. _____

6. _____

I want to encourage you not to use the word 'try' it doesn't inspire commitment. Instead get into the habit of using the word 'choose'. You can then choose to do something or not after assessing the consequences. It's a very powerful word to use with children, to give them a choice of what they want to do and encourages self-responsibility. Also when their choice is actioned it fills them with confidence and they are more committed to the result.

Step 3

Do eliminate the word 'failure' from your vocabulary - it can be quite a liberating experience!

Start thinking of failure as just a different outcome or result to what you had wanted or expected!

Some of your greatest learning will come from these 'different outcomes' so don't deny or ignore them. Rather, celebrate the experience and the learning you have gained. Also make a note of what's good in your life right now. We can sometimes be so focused on what's not good that not only can we miss valuable opportunities but also we miss the good stuff that's actually happening around us!

> How are you? I'm often asked by cashiers and passing acquaintances.
>
> I'm in the habit of saying 'I'm fantastic/fabulous/wonderful', with a smile, which very often causes a smile and a question of 'why?' Even when I'm not so good, I rapidly have to think of justification and something good in my life at that moment. By the time I give them a reason, I'm feeling a lot better and they might share something or just smile – a win/win situation.

What's good in my life now?

Make a list of at least 6 things that are 'good in my life now', more if you can. The more you do the better you will feel. When you think you've completed the list choose to come up with one or two more. The ones that are locked away are the gems!

1. _____

2. _____

3. _____

4. _____

5. _____

6. _____

7. _____

8. _____

Step 4

This Wheel of Life exercise will help you to put some priorities in order and also to look closely at your life at the moment.

In the centre section of the wheel below, write the eight areas of your life that are most important to you. For example; family, children, money, health and vitality, physical environment, friends, partner, fun and recreation, personal development/growth, quality time children/ partner, emotional well-being, social life, spiritual life etc. If you need to, you can add more segments. Can you think of one or two more areas specifically for you?

Give each area a score of between 1-10 as to how you feel about that part of your life right now. For instance 1 is the lowest and might be rated 'catastrophic' and 10 is the highest and might be rated 'fantastic'.

For example:
Business – 6 / Money – 2 / Family – 5 / Partner – 1 / Health – 6 / Fun – 3 / Personal development – 8 / Spiritual – 8
(You can give the same score more than once)

In the middle section of the wheel write one thing that **would greatly enhance** this particular area of your life. Think about what would make it a 10. Or if you've got a score of 10 already, what would make it even better?

For example:
Family - arrange more regular time together
Health - do more regular exercises

In the outer section of the wheel write one thing that you could do right now that would improve this area of your life.

For example:
Family – invite them for Sunday lunch
Health – join a health club

Example Wheel of Life

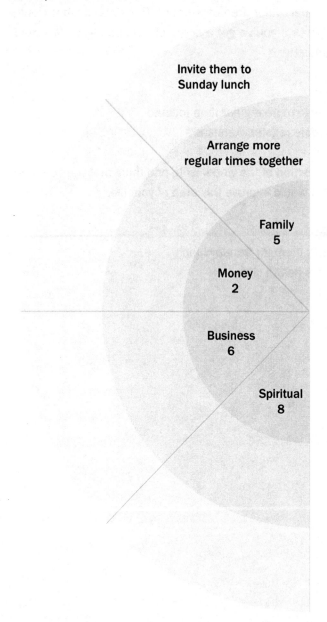

**Invite them to
Sunday lunch**

**Arrange more
regular times together**

**Family
5**

**Money
2**

**Business
6**

**Spiritual
8**

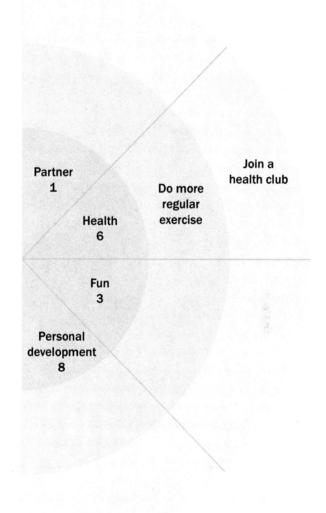

Partner
1

Join a
health club

Do more
regular
exercise

Health
6

Fun
3

Personal
development
8

Your Wheel of Life

I ~~DON'T~~ KNOW YOU ~~ANY~~MORE

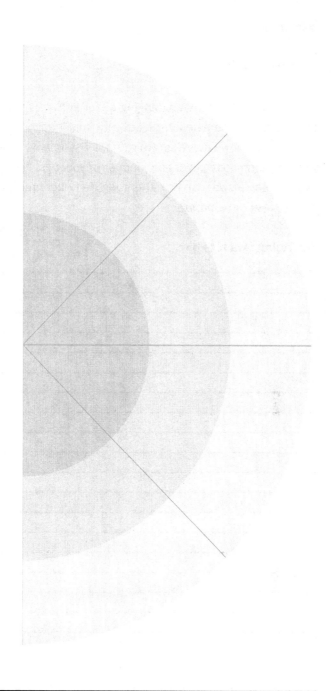

Step 5

Dream time!

Spend at least 20 minutes thinking about and making a list under each of the following headings. Let your imagination run away with you and write down everything in your wildest dreams – most importantly assume no limits of time, money or your age. The 'everything I want to be' answer can be either tangible or not tangible e.g. be a racing driver or be happy.

Everything I want to do

_____
_____
_____
_____
_____
_____
_____
_____
_____
_____
_____
_____
_____
_____
_____
_____
_____
_____
_____

Everything I want to have

_____

_____

_____

_____

_____

_____

_____

_____

_____

_____

_____

_____

_____

_____

_____

_____

_____

_____

_____

_____

_____

_____

_____

_____

_____

_____

_____

_____

_____

_____

Everything I want to be

_____

_____

_____

_____

_____

_____

_____

_____

_____

_____

_____

_____

_____

_____

_____

_____

_____

_____

_____

_____

_____

_____

_____

_____

_____

_____

Step 6

What's important

Pick the six things you most want to do or you resonate with from the combined three lists and write them below (do not worry about the order or priority).

Under each 'want' briefly write how, if you had it now, it would improve your life.

1. Want

_____

_____

_____

_____

How will it improve my life?

_____

_____

_____

_____

_____

_____

_____

2. Want

_____

_____

_____

_____

How will it improve my life?

_____

_____

_____

_____

_____

_____

3. Want

_____

_____

_____

_____

How will it improve my life?

_____

_____

_____

_____

_____

_____

I ~~DON'T~~ KNOW YOU ~~ANY~~MORE

4. Want

_____

_____

_____

_____

How will it improve my life?

_____

_____

_____

_____

_____

_____

5. Want

_____

_____

_____

_____

How will it improve my life?

_____

_____

_____

_____

_____

_____

6. Want

_____

_____

_____

_____

How will it improve my life?

_____

_____

_____

_____

_____

_____

Step 7

Here's how to score

We're now going to figure out which 'want' will have the most positive impact on your life as a whole using the Wheel of Life you completed earlier.

First of all, make a table that has three headings 'Wants' 'Score' and 'Total' across the top and a list down the side from 1 to 6 and list your 'wants'.

Referring back to Your Wheel of Life, ask yourself if you had this 'want' would it improve the individual areas of your life, e.g. Partner, Health, Fun, etc.? Go around the wheel for **EACH area ONE at a time** and ask yourself the same question. If it will, give it 1 point under the 'Score' heading. If it won't improve your life, leave score blank and move on to the next area. **Continue around the wheel until you have gone through all of the areas and entered a score for each.**

Repeat this exercise for 'wants' 2-6. Then add up the scores for each 'want' and enter them under the 'Total' column. Your maximum score can be 8 in this example.

	Wants	Score	Total
1.			
2.			
3.			
4.			
5.			
6.			

You may find that 2 or even 3 'wants' score the same, or there may be one that's way above everything else. Focusing your attention and effort on the highest scoring 'want' will have the greatest positive impact on your life as a whole, and is a great place to start making some changes!

Choose one area to work on initially, then create your SMART goal - see the next chapter.

Remember to get into your most powerful/resourceful state.

Case Study Mrs R

"Before I started the course, I was a person that seemed to get angry and frustrated over the smallest of things, I felt I was overloaded with work and kids and finding it really hard to juggle everything and consequently letting myself and the people around me down, which resulted in arguments.

I could see the effects of this on my children and how they responded to a situation, which was to shout, there seemed to be a real lack of respect and communication in our family and I just felt myself going around in circles and didn't really enjoy life. I wanted to break this circle but did not know how.

When I saw the advert for the Course, it felt like someone had read my mind; I rang to sign up straight away. It took me a couple of weeks to open up to the rest of the group and really express myself deeply and I believe this was due to believing others would judge me and my situation, but as time went on, I realized everyone in the group was in the same boat, my trust grew and it was a relief to talk about my situation and I came out of the course feeling empowered and knowing I could change my situation.

The course has helped me by firstly looking at myself and changing things about myself. Just making small changes has had such an impact on my family life. The two most important tools I have gained from this course were listening and changing my thought process. I have learnt to listen to my children, actually energetic

---

listening, sitting there and really getting to know what they're trying to say and trying to understand it by asking them open questions, which help them to express themselves a lot more which helped them to communicate and express their feelings and emotions, I in return would also open up and express how I felt about things.

The second tool was to change my thought process, just understanding I could change my thought process at any time and react differently to situations, for instance instead of shouting, I could just walk away, calm down and then deal with the situation, I found this quite hard to do, but, reflecting on situations that I have used this skill in, makes me more determined to continue.

Towards the end of the course I felt that things weren't a problem and more of a challenge, which can be overcome. I have changed my way of thinking and don't worry about the small things anymore, changing me has changed my husband and children. It is also a challenge to continue with the changes as it's so easy to fall back into your old ways, that's why I feel the weekly Family Coaching Café is a great idea as it gives you a boost and reminds you of where you were and where you are now.

It is also provides opportunities to make a difference to other people, by talking about your situation and to show them how far you have come and that they could achieve the same."
Mrs R

CHAPTER 3

Creating a SMART goal

*Whether you think you can, or you
think you can't - you're right.*
Henry Ford

SMART goals

SMART is an acronym for Specific, Measurable, Achievable, Realistic
and Tangible/Timed.

Your goals must contain all of these elements to make them valuable
and enable you to make progress and achieve. While this process
is very common, it's not always totally understood, even by some
professionals. The most common areas of misunderstanding are:

1. Specific – the goal only involves you

2. Measurable – the goal must be able to be measured by someone
    else and

3. Tangible. "To be happier" is not tangible. The question is "what
    can you do that would make you happier" and then create a goal
    around that? So let's go through each of them in turn

Specific

A specific goal has a much greater chance of being accomplished than a general goal. To set a specific goal you must answer the following questions:

Who: Who is involved? It must only involve you.

What: What is it I want to accomplish?

Where: Where will I be?

When: When do I want it by? If it's a big goal, does it need to be broken down into steps?

Which: Which things will help me and which will hold me back?

Why: Why do I want this? (Be specific!) What will I see, hear, feel when I have achieved my goal?

Example: A general goal would be, 'get in shape' but a specific goal would be 'lose 5lbs within 30 days and be able to run for 10 minutes at the gym'.

Measurable

When you measure your progress, you stay on track, reach your target dates and experience the exhilaration of achievement that spurs you on to the continued effort required to reach your goal. Ask yourself 'How will I know when I've achieved it?' and write it down. Remember it must be able to be measured by someone else.

Achievable

When you identify the goals that are most important to you, you start to find ways to make them come true. You also begin to develop the attitudes, abilities and skills to reach them. In addition you will start to notice previously overlooked opportunities. These can bring you closer to achieving your goals. Some questions that can help are:

1. What could I do to move myself one step forward?

2. What would I be doing if:
   I were not answerable to anyone
   I had all the money in the world
   I could devote all my time to this

3. What could I do if I did not have to live with the consequences?

4. If I secretly knew what I should do first, what would it be?

5. Review options carefully - does this spark another idea? The more options the better, so don't rush

Choose one option that will move you forward. It can be the easiest, cheapest, and quickest. Confirm that it will move you forward. What will the benefit be? Identify it and write it down.

Plan your steps wisely and establish a time frame that stretches you but is not out of reach.

Goals that you may once have thought would never happen move closer and become attainable. This is not because your goals shrink but because you grow and expand to match them. When you list your goals, you build your self-image.

Realistic

To be realistic, a goal must be something which you are both willing and able to work towards. A goal can be both high and realistic; you are the only one who can decide just how high your goal should be. But be sure that every goal represents measurable progress.

Tangible/Timed

A goal is tangible when you can experience it with one of the senses. In your mind, can you see a picture of it, hear someone congratulating you on achieving it, taste the success, or smell something new? If you can, you have a better chance of making it specific and measurable and thus attainable. (Timed has been covered under 'Specific')

You must feel excited and really want this goal otherwise it's not going to happen.

My goal is to:

_____

_____

_____

_____

A note of caution

To ensure your success, all the attributes of a SMART goal must be in place. In addition, you may want to consider the following points if you have a big or intangible/emotional goal.

A big goal

If your goal is a big goal, for example 'I want to lose 2 stone in weight'.

1. Make an Action Plan and break the goal down into smaller steps

2. These steps must still contain all the attributes of a SMART goal

3. You may find, as you get closer to the next step your progress is faster and you may need to revise the future steps

An intangible/emotional goal

If your goal is emotional, for example 'I want to be happier'.

1. We know from 'T' Tangible/Timed that you cannot have an intangible goal

2. To make progress on this type of goal, you need to define what 'happier' means for you

3. By defining the goal it becomes tangible. For example 'happier' might be spending more quality time with your children

4. You can now create your SMART goal

Challenge your goal

Any goal that is worthwhile has to be a challenge. Could you review your goal and increase it by a value of about 10%?

My revised goal is:

_____

_____

_____

_____

Rate your goal and commit

By now, you should be raring to get going with your new goal. But, before you do, stop and ask yourself if this is what you really want and give it a score of between 1-10 (where 1 means that you're not bothered either way and 10 is a 'must have').

If you're not scoring at least a 9, you need to go back a few steps and find a goal that you really do want. Or consider how you can change the basis of this goal whilst retaining the attraction and motivation to increase the score to a 10.

I love doing this exercise in a group, because when I connect to the person working on their goal I get a real sense of how authentic they are with their scoring. And, if it's way different from what I sense, I say, "Can I be honest? I'm not getting the same feeling as you. Is there something I'm missing?" Inevitably, this will throw up a revised score or different goal.

But what really amazes people is that all the others in the group have a similar sense of the authentic score when they are asked - true energetic connection in practice.

The Law of Attraction – the missing element!

One of the Laws of the Universe is the 'Law of Attraction'. This basically says, "What you focus on is what you get". So, if you are looking for the magnificence in someone that is what you will see. The opposite is true.

There is a great film and a book "The Secret", which is all about the Law of Attraction. It's fabulous because it's created so much awareness of this law. The down side is that a lot of people thought they just had to think about something and it would arrive in their lap. I think there wasn't enough emphasis on taking inspired action as well. Which is why the Law of Attraction works so well alongside the logical SMART goal process.

On completion of your goal, remember to celebrate your achievement.

Celebrate your success

This is the best part. Be good to yourself. Enjoy your success and celebrate in a special way. During your celebration take some time to think back on what you have achieved!

Write down everything you saw, heard and felt when you were successful - and keep it near you to remind yourself. If you do not use a journal, perhaps now is a good time to start one?

Celebrating success is critical, it is equally important to remember that there is no failure - only feedback and learning. What have you learnt from this experience? What can you do differently next time?

To make way for this goal, it sometimes helps to review your time commitment. But remember, it's no good cheating yourself because that is probably what stopped you achieving what you wanted in the past.

If it didn't happen

If you weren't successful reflect on the progress you've made towards your goal. You may have got further than you have before - that's success in itself. If desirable, you can gently look at some possible reasons:

1. What is holding you back from achieving your goal?
   Was it the action of someone else that sabotaged you?

2. How important is the goal for you right now?
   It must be a real 'must have' goal

3. What needs to happen so that you can achieve your goal?

4. How is not achieving your goal affecting you?

A very empowering word is – NO. It creates a completely different perspective for the person approaching you and can create some extra time for you. Choose to do it sometimes, but be gentle in how you use it, others may not be expecting it!

I (name) _____rate my goal a 10.

My goal is to:

_____

_____

_____

_____

_____

_____

Signed

_____

Date

_____

You are on a roll

During your celebration, make the most of this euphoric period by going back to review your Wheel of Life.

Before creating the next SMART goal you will want to review your scoring process to ascertain whether things have changed now you are in different circumstances - it usually does!

The next chapter has a great exercise to lock in this euphoric feeling and resourceful state.

Case Study Miss JM

"When I started the course I was at an extreme low. I had such negative beliefs about nearly every aspect of my life. Steered away from most friends, thinking they disliked me or judged how I parented. I did not enjoy going to work as I felt I was incapable and out of touch where I had gone to a part time member of the team. I felt that leaving my son in childcare was the wrong option and selfish of me, he was acting out in day care hitting other children, which made me think that this setting wasn't the right one.

My partner works full time and takes every bit of overtime available, so often I was tired and stressed. My partner would often just want to sit and rest and take time to himself, I would then allow my thoughts to become negative and think he no longer wanted to be a member our little family unit. Basically, I was in need of some serious positivity and empowerment and needed to change how I let my thoughts affect my behaviour.

Where I was in such a negative cycle, I was oblivious to the fact that my son was absorbing my negativity and sensing my sadness, even though I wasn't displaying it in an obvious manner. My general persona was evident enough, although I was ignorant to this. My son would be crying and displaying anger to which I thought was for no reason at all whilst I sat thinking about how unhappy I was. At times I would think my son's behaviour was a reaction to my incompetence of parenting!

Now I have attended the Parent Champion course and discovered that by concentrating on my own magnificence and capabilities, I now enjoy every aspect of my life. My son's behaviour has had a complete turnaround. I now parent naturally, I'm not in my head thinking about repercussions or what other people think, I actually enjoy the moment and allow my son to choose, explore and discover the consequences. This approach has developed him so much. He really has become a beautiful character and has a real sense of empowerment which is evident in his behaviour, not only at home, but in day care also.

This course has taken me out of my comfort zone completely and taught me to always be open-minded and non-judgemental and this has all been good! I am a new person with new ambitions and goals – such a positive contrast to before I attended the course. So if ever you have the opportunity to attend the course - I would say it is a must!"
Miss JM

CHAPTER 4

The power of thought

If you can imagine it,
You can achieve it.
If you can dream it,
You can become it.
William Arthur Ward

You may not realise how powerful your thoughts are. They create your reality and affect your feelings, emotions and behaviour.

Thinking is a universal function like breathing. However, we all process thoughts differently because we are all unique individuals living within our own unique circumstances. As we are these unique individuals, the power we give to different thoughts can create diverse opinions of how we see a situation or object. How often have you had a different interpretation of what someone says or a difference of opinion about what he or she likes and you don't?

It all stems from thought.

The good news is that, because your thoughts drive your feelings, emotions, behaviour and reactions, a change in your thought can bring about a change in your behaviour.

Sometimes, we feel as though we are bombarded by our thoughts. We can change this by realising and accepting that we can control our thoughts – easier to say than do but another liberating exercise. It's also our choice how we react to our thoughts – we all have free will.

Thoughts do not mean anything until we give them power. If you don't like what you are thinking, choose another thought. You can only think and empower one thought at a time!

Consider the different effect on a relationship: instead of Mum, it could be Dad, carer, brother, sister or friend, in each of the following scenarios!

Scenario A - Unhappy

I am a creature of habit. I love to start my day with Special K in the mornings. I'm feeling unhappy so everything looks dark, bleak and miserable. I come down the stairs, open the fridge and find no milk. My daughter comes into the room bright and bubbly and I snap back with "leave me alone".

Scenario B - Happy

I am a creature of habit. I love to start my day with Special K in the mornings. I'm feeling happy so everything looks great. I notice the sun is shining, my favourite tune is on the radio, I come down stairs, open the fridge and find no milk. I think 'Oh well I'll have some toast for a change.' My daughter comes into the room and we have a great conversation and decide to do something special together at the weekend.

Two completely different outcomes created by different thoughts. So, how does a thought work?

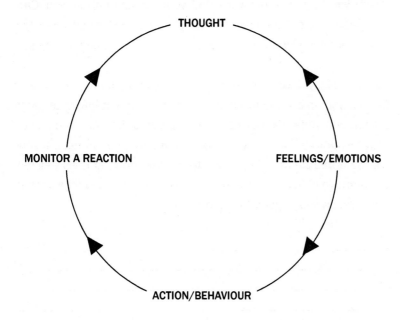

Our thoughts drive our feelings, behaviour and reactions. You can change your thoughts; therefore you can change your behaviour.

You can copy and complete the worksheet on the following pages.

Reference: see the work of Sydney Banks at www.sydneybanks.org

---

Worksheet – Thought

I want you to notice this week how your thoughts affect you. Can you make a note of some of the unexpected good/wonderful things that happened when you were actually expecting a bad situation?

For example, you were expecting your son/daughter to come home from school in a bad mood. So you decided to get into your most resourceful state and having a relaxing cup of tea and listening to your favourite music. They did come home in a bad mood but saw you were relaxed and they chose to be in a good mood as well. So the purpose of this exercise is to find out what the thought was that encouraged you to get into a good mood.

1. _____
   _____
   _____
   _____
   _____
   _____
   _____

2. _____
   _____
   _____
   _____
   _____
   _____

3. _____

_____

_____

_____

_____

_____

_____

I appreciate it is not easy to monitor your thoughts, especially in the heat of the moment, but if you saw the value in it, you may be tempted to do it more often and even make a habit of it!

You are in control of your thoughts, your feelings, your behaviour and, therefore, your actions. You are creating your own reality.

Case Study Mrs S

"I have listened intently to everyone on the course and have learnt so much about people and our thoughts, feelings and behaviour, but most of all it's made me look at my own life and re-value it. Before the course my thoughts were always negative, it felt like I had got myself into a rut and it was easy to let my feelings and emotions get the better of me.

I thought that I wasn't coping and dealing very well with certain situations that occurred in my life and I doubted myself, I was alone a lot and felt trapped in my own little world and I didn't want anyone to invade my space (it made me feel threatened).

I was praised from time to time by my family and those close to me, but my own thoughts made it hard for me to accept this. Like many other people I'm a single parent and have bought up my five daughters on my own, it wasn't easy asking myself if I was doing and saying the right things and making decisions on my own.

However, I have learnt enough to know that my thoughts are more positive now than ever before. I do have the occasional time when things get me down but I let my thoughts change that. Deep down I know that I did my best for my children while I was bringing them up and I know they appreciate that.

Those situations that I thought I wasn't coping with, well I was and if anything I would say that I have learnt a lot from them and I'm a stronger and better person. I take time now to listen to my thoughts and my children express their own. Things have changed at home, my youngest daughter tells me how she is feeling, what she wants to do and say and expresses herself much more. I have found that her older sisters listen to her and take into consideration what she has to say and what she wants to do more, rather than just give orders."

Mrs S

CHAPTER 5

This is where the magic begins

What lies behind us and lies before us are small matters compared to what lies within us. And when we bring what is within out into the world, miracles happen.
Henry David Thoreau

By now you will have started to feel more in control of your life. You might also have noticed a reference to the 'energetic connection', so you are in the right place to talk about the sensitivity of children. We've mentioned that teens will provide a bigger challenge because they have been exposed to more negativity and self-doubt, but they will still have the same potential to connect, some more so. Choose to be patient and your patience will be paid back in ways you never thought possible.

You might have noticed your children can sense the mood you're in before you enter a room? I wanted a generic term for this type of 'connection', so I've been using the phrase 'energetic connection'. It can also be described as intuition, instincts, gut feeling, sensual awareness, knowing, love and what Neuroscience is explaining as our interconnectedness with everyone. This energetic connection can have profound implications for our personal relationships.

Have you noticed :

- When you enter a room full of strangers you can feel comfortable or uncomfortable?

- Someone saying, "I was just thinking of that" or you have said it yourself?

- If the phone rings and it's someone you haven't seen or heard of for sometime, but you've been thinking about them?

- You can sense someone behind you without hearing them?

Then you have experienced that 'energy' and it's always there for you to access. This energy has a huge impact on the quality of a connection between two people and the parents we have worked with have noticed that children are infinitely more sensitive.

You know how when you're feeling relaxed, it can feel like you're more able to instinctively know what it is your baby wants? I believe this is because when we are relaxed we can more easily pick up on the energy that flows between us and others.

Our use of the term energetic connection is a simplification of the connection between science and spirituality. The work of Dr Claude Swanson is the most comprehensive and easy to understand reference I've found on the subject, the more open minded you are, the more you will take from his work.

The biggest influence on your potential to connect energetically is how good you feel about yourself.

When you feel good about yourself everything feels easier - the children are happier and more content, but when you're angry or stressed the opposite is true. When your emotions are up in the air or you're focussing on your problems, you're very unlikely to have a positive connection.

I believe there is huge potential in this positive energetic connection.

Developing awareness of these experiences opens up the possibilities of the positive energetic connection in your relationships. Why is this important? These are some of the more obvious reasons:

- It helps you realise you can trust your instincts/intuition/sensing/knowing more.

- It helps you realise how sensitive your children are, how innately connected they are and how even thoughts are transmitted.

- Children with labels - 'learning difficulties', 'dyslexia', 'A.S.D' are likely to be even more sensitive to others energy.

- There's a growing body of evidence showing how children take responsibility for their parents' emotional state.

- By making children aware of this energetic connection, they can trust their innate abilities and have confidence in themselves.

- By encouraging children to explore their energetic connection with others, they are opening up a whole world of possibilities and opportunities.

Here are some examples from parents:

Ms K a single Mum, with a son of 4 years old has global development delay, and she can now communicate non-verbally which has transformed communication within the family unit.

Ms J was explaining to her (two your old) son that his daddy was leaving the family home and she was a little sad about it. Her son then replied, "oh mummy I'm so happy" and then went onto say "don't worry mummy I'll get you a present and your be so happy".

Ms S single Mum, with a 7-year-old son diagnosed with ADHD has been sending loving energy to her son whilst he is at school. Her sons teacher pulled her to one side when she went to collect him and said how much of a fantastic day he had, and that at one point when his usual group of friends became disruptive, he took himself away from them and played with another group of children. Mum proudly explained that he now even makes eye contact with people.

Mrs A was explaining that she had a horrible dream in the week and it upset her which, she knows is silly; however she was ironing one morning and for some reason she thought about the dream again and felt emotional. Her son (aged 4) looked up at her from playing and said, "mummy are you ok" Mum asked "What made you ask me that" and he replied "I thought you felt sad" he then asked "are you feeling ok now mummy".

Mrs AM said that she had been thinking about her deceased mother. She said that she had a sensation on the back of her neck and when speaking to her daughter later in the day it transpired that she too had also had the same thoughts and feelings.

Miss GW I had a dream of my Nan chatting to me but only remembered the last bit she told me, which was to get out of bed and close the balcony door. I woke up a bit confused as I don't normally remember my dreams', went to check on the door and it was open a couple of inches.

Mrs SS looks in on her children at night and her son was fast asleep snoring and she sent a message energetically to say that she loved him and he sat up without waking and said "I love you mummy" and laid down again, she was so surprised that she had trouble sleeping.

Miss LH said that when she went to look at the venue of a place where she is getting married, there was a skate park behind it and sensed that her young son would want to go afterwards. Normally she wouldn't of let him go as he is small. She asked him if he wanted to go in there, which he did. While he was in there she turned to talk to her partner, she sensed that she had to turn round. At that point her son was in another skater's path so she shouted to warn him of the danger.

Miss PJ said I had a thought – I need to pick her blanket up. Without asking she did it and gave it to me.

Miss JM said that on the day she went to the beach that she had to meet up with her brother before hand. She sensed that something was wrong and that her brother was late. She heard a screech of a car and ran out to see what had happened. A man had collapsed in front of her brother's car and he had to swerve round him. She just knew that something was going to happen.

Mrs VC said by connecting with my 2nd child (who has a speech and hearing problem) her speech has become much better, I understand her more and there are less tantrums.

Mrs KC said she was going out and her son insisted on wearing a sun hat that totally clashed with what he was wearing (plus it wasn't sunny!). I was sitting next to him in the back of the car thinking 'how can I get that off him before we get there'. He turned to me and said 'I like my hat Mummy, I not taking it off'!

Mrs KF said that she had a connection while at the hospital when she saw the look in her daughter's eyes, she looked scared. She said that she gave a look back to say you're safe and ok and her daughter started to look more relaxed and had a glint in her eyes.

Mrs AR said that she had bought her daughter a guinea pig as a pet and when she met her daughter from school she seemed happier than usual and said 'mummy have you bought me a bunny?' She said it was as if she was reading my thoughts, not a bunny but yes a pet.

Mrs KC said her son connected with Nan and said 'Nannie garden'. Later she phoned her Mum and it transpired that his Nan was thinking of going out into the garden at that time — it spooked her and her Nan!

Mrs AB was thinking it would be nice if her husband offered to take a turn in the bath time ritual for a change - and he did!

Miss SK got up made the breakfast, getting ready and thinking that her son's room needed cleaning, a few minutes later he came out of the room having cleaned it!

Talking about feelings, I'm reminded that when someone says something profound to me, or I say something profound, I get a tingling sensation and the more profound the bigger the tingle. Other people have different 'sensing' experiences; you just need to be aware of the possibility, and then explore how you connect energetically.

This book is written to encourage you to try different exercises to find how you connect energetically and so get into your most resourceful state - at will. It can take some practice but I can absolutely guarantee it's worth it.

I've talked about our personal development approach being different from regular 'parenting skills' and how we accept that everyone has the answers they need inside. What is required is the breakthrough question to unlock the answer. I've noticed when I'm in my most resourceful state and connected to someone I get a sense of what the next question is – it's a fantastic feeling of contentment and connection.

When you are in your most resourceful state and set the intention to connect with someone who is equally relaxed, receptive and open, you will connect a whole new world of possibilities!!! This is magic in action.

Remember the most exciting part of all this. You will be able to teach your children these fantastic skills, which will unlock a whole new life for them. And it's so much easier, even natural for them to connect.

Some pointers and preparation to consider when you are communicating/connecting:

- Get into a resourceful state. Focus on your passion, what drives you - feel fantastic

- Set the intention for the best possible outcome

- Imagine the room being full of positivity

- Interact with the magnificent version of the person in front of you

- Don't worry about an emotional reaction; it indicates someone is ready to change something

- Be transparent with your agenda, and open to whatever wants to happen

- Trust you have done your very best and allow it to show up in ways you couldn't possibly imagine

- And, most important of all - always trust your intuition/instincts/gut feeling and have loads of fun and laughter along the way.

As you progress on your own personal development path everyone around you will notice – they may not say anything or even believe it but slowly it will happen. Realise you are changing the habits of a lifetime, so be gentle with yourself. There will be times when you slip back and that's OK because those times will get shorter and shorter as you evolve and become more empowered.

The younger your children are the easier it is to make that connection and the older we get the more difficult it is. Adults have more life experiences and since we are brought up in a world of negativity we tend to close down our feelings, sometimes because it's safer, or we believe it is. The end result is that we tend not to try new things because we believe we might fail.

Children, on the other hand, are full of fun and joy. They're always experimenting and learning new things. You can tap into this enthusiasm when you connect with your child on that level.

During workshops I do what I call an 'expansion' exercise. This is a guided visualisation to help clear your mind and connect you with your essence. If you would like to experience it I have posted a version on YouTube, search for "Parents meditation".

In 2006, I ran a Conference "Kids are really different these days... pioneering an evolutionary world" and Dr Graham Taylor wrote a report. This gives another perspective on the 'energetic connection', it's included as Appendix III.

Don't worry if this all sounds a bit too esoteric. Thousands of parents from all walks of life have found it has transformed their lives and those of their families.

If you're open to more about energy read on.

Case Study Mrs GW

"Before I started the course I couldn't handle my emotions and it had a knock on effect on my daughter. She was only 2 but always saw me sad, upset and not understanding why. As a very young child up until my teens I was sexually and physically abused, which left me with a lot of scars and very emotional.

In my early teens I turned to drink and drugs to numb my pain, flash backs and emotions, which were my tools to cope as I felt dirty, powerless, ashamed etc. When I fell pregnant with my daughter I gave up the drink and drugs straight away but the emotions of my childhood crept back in and I knew I couldn't go back to drink and drugs to numb my pain, flash backs and emotions.

I went through counseling about a year ago which helped me use tools to conquer the flash backs etc but I still had the pain and emotions. I started to isolate myself and stayed in my shell, which was not good for me or my daughter. At this stage I knew I had to do something to move me to living for now and make me love myself again and be happy, to start living and not just existing.

What I take from this course is I have now been able to trust people again. I have made new friends and started to go to a group that I'm interested in.

I am now more confident and most of all I can see the magnificent me and have grown to love myself again. I have also just got myself a job to work with young offenders in which I intend to use the tools and lessons in mentoring them and helping them believe in their selves so that they can change their lives.

I can now walk away from negativity and feel more empowered. I no longer hang my head down in shame; I hold my head up high, as I'm a survivor. My daughter is much happier now and our home life is more fun, full of happiness and love. I'm a more positive person now and believe that I can achieve anything I set my mind to. I'm really looking forward to the new me and the next chapter in my life."

Ms GW

PS   Ms GW is doing a sponsored Skydive on behalf of our charity Every Family Matters

PPS   During the course Ms GW set a goal to overcome her isolation and get out more - she did and has now met a man she has become engaged to and plans to get married next year.

CHAPTER 6

More about energy

Learn to let go.
That is the key to happiness
Buddha

I see energy as a hidden force in all of us and everything in our lives. We've all sensed if a person approaching is a friend or foe, or we get a feeling that something is going to be good or bad when we walk into a strange situation.

When I started life coaching, I realised that intuition was a magic ingredient and that, if I could connect with it, I could use it with incredible results for the benefit of my clients. Because I had an interest in alternative therapies I explored connecting at a deeper level and the first thing I learnt was that, before we do any energy work, we need to relax, quieten our minds and take a few slow deep breaths. So I began to meditate.

Meditation

More and more people are adding some kind of meditation to their daily routine, either as an effective antidote to stress or as a simple method of relaxation. It enables you to create new attitudes and responses to life, giving you a clearer spiritual understanding of yourself.

Meditation is the process of re-discovering, enjoying and using the positive qualities already latent within you. Like any skill, meditation requires practice to achieve positive and satisfying results. By doing a little every day, it soon becomes a natural and easy habit, which generously rewards you for the modest effort it involved.

Exercise

1. Make an appointment with yourself for 10-20 minutes each morning or evening.

2. Find a quiet place and relax. Subdued light and soft music can create an appropriate atmosphere.

3. Sit comfortably upright on the floor or in a chair.

4. Keep your eyes open and, without staring, gently rest them on a chosen point somewhere in front of you in the room.

5. Gently withdraw your attention from all sights and sounds.

6. Become the observer of your own thoughts.

7. Don't try to stop thinking; just be the observer. Don't judge or get carried away by your own thoughts, just watch.

8. Gradually they will slow down and you will begin to feel more peaceful.

9. Create one thought for yourself, about yourself; for example, "I am a peaceful being".

10. Hold that thought on the screen of your mind; visualise yourself being peaceful, quiet and still.

11. Stay as long as you can in the awareness of that thought. Don't fight any other thoughts or memories that may come to distract you. Just watch them pass by and return to your created thought, "I am a peaceful being".

12. Acknowledge and appreciate the positive feelings and other positive thoughts, which may spring directly from this one thought.

13. Be stable in these feelings for a few minutes. Be aware of unrelated thoughts.

14. Finish your meditation by closing your eyes for a few moments and creating complete silence in your mind.

The more you do this the more you will get from it – and it's well worth the time investment. I found that meditation opened the door for a deeper connection to my intuition.

I was fortunate to enjoy a retreat in Oxfordshire organised by the Brahma Kumaris World Spiritual University, who supplied the exercise.

One of their practices is to use 'traffic control' – on the hour, every hour, for a few minutes relaxing music is played and everyone stops what they are doing and centres themselves. I found it most relaxing and so, when I'm working from home, I use a kitchen timer and every hour I stop for a couple of minutes. I find when I go back to my work I'm refreshed and see things from a different perspective. Try it when you can.

Energy exercises

A couple of simple energy exercises:

1 - Testing energy

Ask someone to extend their arm out straight by the side of them. Ask them to show some resistance, close their eyes and think about someone or something they have very strong negative feelings for. You see how much strength it takes to push their hand down to their side.

Now ask them to do the same, with the same resistance but think about someone they really love. You will find they are much stronger this time. It proves we are stronger physically when we feel good inside.

2 - Managing energy as an emotion (based on the work of Sylvia Hartmann[1])

This is an exercise in moving energy. The existence of subtle energy was well known to ancient traditions. For instance, the Chinese built their health care around it with acupuncture. We are going to unblock energy channels that will allow energy to flow and thereby relieve symptoms. I love this story!

A client phoned me (I am an Energy practitioner) from France. She was having a panic attack and was desperate. I asked, "Now you are having your panic attack, where do you feel it in your body?" She said, "In my chest." I said, "That is just blocked energy, soften it with your intention and just let it flow." I waited and then asked,

"What is happening to that blockage? Is it moving?" She said, "It is moving into my neck." I said, "Is there any left in your chest?"

She said, "A little." I said, "Just keep softening it. It is only blocked energy, just let it flow." She said, "It is in my neck and shoulders now" I said, "Where is it the strongest?" She said, "In my neck." I said, "Just soften it and let it flow". She said, "It is moving down my arms - oh! My husband is coming, I don't want him to know about this!" I said, "You know what to do. Just go to the lavatory and keep softening the energy and let it flow until the problem has gone."

An unfortunate choice of venue for softening and letting it flow! BUT:

---

1 Reference: from EMOTRANCE an energy-based therapy, the brainchild of Sylvia Hartmann, one of the foremost pioneers in Meridian Energy Therapies

---

She called a day later to say her panic attack had gone and that was amazing. I guess she had learnt the process and just did it!

Try this exercise with your partner or friend – when it is appropriate.

One be the Energy Practitioner (EP), the other be the Client, and find an issue that is a current challenge. Facilitate the unblocking of energy by repeating the script (see above bold italic wording) until the issue no longer causes a problem. Swap roles and repeat.

Note that you are only facilitating the unblocking of energy. Let it flow and just ask, from time to time, "Where is it now?" Hear the reply, say, "Fine, just let it flow." If it stops somewhere say, "Just soften it and let it flow, it is only blocked energy, until it has gone (wherever)."

Then test - "When you think of (the issue), what happens?" If the feeling comes back, repeat the process until the Client cannot get the problem back.

I want to tell you about a book 'Messages from Water' by Masaru Emoto. He has studied the effect of music, words, thought, consciousness etc. on water crystals. Basically, negative influences create ugly-shaped crystals, while positive influences create beautiful crystal images.

This was graphically highlighted for me when I looked at some photographs of crystals with both positive and negative associations. The difference in appearance was striking.

Those with positive associations e.g. 'thank you', 'love', 'appreciation' and 'angel' were beautifully shaped, while those with negative connotations such as 'you fool', 'devil', 'you make me sick' and 'I'll kill you' were quite distorted and ugly.

As our body is made up mostly of water – approximately 85% of your brain, 80% of your blood and 70% of your muscles are water – you can see that your thoughts have a profound effect on your body. You can, perhaps, also see how important water is to you and why you should take care not to become dehydrated.

A huge step forward is to shake off that negativity and see how you can focus on your successes, so read on.

Case Study Miss E

"I was in a really bad place with my three children, I'm a single Mum and they were all under five at the time and every day was a struggle. My partner was dependent on prescribed medication and he also liked a drink and that wasn't a good mix. His behaviour was erratic and I never knew what he was going to do next. I was in fear for my children.

My life was hell just trying to keep everything normal for the children and my own sanity. I ended up going to the doctors for anti-depressants. I felt I was out of control and felt incompetent in being a Mum. It was so bad I just wanted someone to take them away – for good.

It was my family support worker who recognised my vulnerability and suggested the course. At first I was dead against it, I didn't want anyone to know I needed help and was too proud to ask for it. And I thought I could manage anyway.

In the end they nagged me enough to give it a try. After the first session I thought it's not for me. Then when I thought about it afterwards I realised there were others in the same dark place and what have I got to lose.

I think one of the biggest things is coming to terms with yourself in the way of believing in yourself and you can do it, it's just being given the right tools to do it with.

Once I learned to believe in myself and I am doing the right thing, not coming from your head but it's what you feel, that's what's right and what's wrong.

I've got to think about myself. I'm just so much happier within myself. So much happier within my family life. My children are so much happier. I dance around the kitchen, singing or trying to and every day is a joy.

There's always going to be times when you think ahhh this isn't going to go well but then if you just practice what you've learned you can't go wrong. And if I hadn't of done the course, I don't know where I would be to this day. I don't think I'd still be standing.

I think that's what really amazed me as well though because you sit there and you think I don't know about anyone else but I thought it was just me feeling like this I thought everyone was happy in their lives. But coming to the course, you realize, God it's everybody.

I think my tools were the expansion exercise, just focusing on one thing instead of a thousand different ones going around at the same time and listening as well because I thought I listened, I really did, during washing up, yeah that's nice, that's nice. But I wasn't anywhere near it.

Actually in-depth listening, getting to the root of it, the heart of it, it's such a difference. I thought it was that they weren't listening to me, that they weren't doing what I wanted them to do. And you learn it's not that they're not listening to you, it's you're not actually listening to them. The way I did that was listening and finding out about them as individuals, not as my children but as their own person and how wonderful they are.

For me, the value is being, knowing that I was in that place where new parents are now thinking, ... no one can help me.

And sometimes it's nice to reflect on that, not to forget you were there once. And reassurance that if you listen to yourself, connect with yourself, it will work out. You may not see the benefits of it straightway, but over time and they're big, big benefits. To know I'm helping somebody, I'm able to, I'm confident enough to without thinking. It may not work for them every time but it worked and it's sharing, sharing what worked. Trial and error.

I have a more understanding response to my children and a much better relationship. We talk, laugh and play more than we ever did, I love everything about my girls and I am a great Mum."
Miss E

CHAPTER 7

Success breeds success

Everything's in the mind.
That's where it all starts.
Knowing what you want is the
first step toward getting it.
Mae West

Because of all the negativity we are surrounded by we need to make a choice to look for and record the successes/achievements/improvements in our life.

Do you know a child hears 'no' over 400 times a day and 'yes' only 20? By the time we have experienced a few years of adulthood we are brainwashed into thinking we 'can't do anything' and we are 'no good at anything' it is no wonder we find it difficult to break out of a rut or have perseverance to try something new. Perhaps this is also the reason we find it difficult to accept a compliment!

We want to continue to help you making changes in your life, so let's start recording our successes, wins, achievements or improvements. For some, it may be necessary instead of a success to look for the 'nicest thing that happened' today. For others, it may be they are so low that everything looks bleak. Often just chatting and lightening the mood loosens things and slowly a 'gem' will reveal itself – and a light goes on.

Start by recording the date, time, details of the success or 'nice thing that happened'. Next are the feelings and emotions associated to the event, it's really important to record these so that, when we are down, we can recreate these lovely nice warm feelings to give us a lift. When you concentrate on these sensations they can really change your mood.

With children, it's really helpful to get them to talk about their feelings and locate where they are in their body.

Finally, what is the potential for this success? For example, if a child swims a width of a pool for the first time, ask, "What is the potential or what will you be able to do next?" One answer might be, "I will swim a length next time". Another might be, "I will win a gold medal in the next Olympics". You just never know what other people think, feel or believe and what their version of success might be.

My Success Diary

Day, date and time   What did you achieve?

_____   _____

_____   _____

_____   _____

_____   _____

_____   _____

_____   _____

_____   _____

_____   _____

_____   _____

_____   _____

_____   _____

_____   _____

_____   _____

_____   _____

_____   _____

_____   _____

_____   _____

_____   _____

_____   _____

_____   _____

_____   _____

How did you feel about that, what were your feelings and emotions in your body?

What is your potential now, what else can you achieve?

_____   _____
_____   _____
_____   _____
_____   _____
_____   _____
_____   _____
_____   _____
_____   _____
_____   _____
_____   _____
_____   _____
_____   _____
_____   _____
_____   _____
_____   _____
_____   _____
_____   _____
_____   _____
_____   _____
_____   _____
_____   _____
_____   _____
_____   _____

Celebrate success

What I've found particularly powerful in family coaching is to get each family member to do their own diaries and, at the end of the week, to have a sharing session where they can all celebrate each other's achievements. It's amazing how much they don't know about each other's challenges and successes.

It's very important to celebrate successes. It's all too easy to look up the mountain to see how far we still have to go instead of looking back to see how far we've come.

Celebration doesn't have to be massive or expensive; just something to mark the event. For Mum, it might be a lovely long bath with scented candles or perhaps she'd like a large box of chocolates! For a young person it might be some extra time spent with a best friend. During the celebration, relive those wonderful feelings and sensations you had originally.

A real treat is to look back in a month's time and re-read some of the entries. Not only will it give you a 'lift', it will reinforce how far you've come. Yipeeee!

Case Study Miss K

"When I started the course, I was a very negative person, if anything was going right I would always think it was going to go wrong. But not now I always look at the positives because if I have it in my mind that everything is going to go wrong then it most likely will.

I see now that if I want something good to happen then I have to think good.

Another thing that I wasn't very good at before I started was listening to my daughter, she's not even two yet, so sometimes I can't understand what she is saying and to be honest I didn't really listen. Since this course I have learnt there are different levels of listening and I was listening at the worst level. Now I listen in the best way and have learnt that she says so much that actually does make sense. I now have little conversations with her.

When I had my daughter I thought that I didn't matter anymore, that I had to think of just her and put how I feel aside, I now know that if I think of myself as well then she benefits from it just as much as I do.

Before the course, I wasn't very confident around new people, I would keep myself to myself, not express my opinions or feelings. Also I would never stand in front of people and speak publicly, but in the last eight weeks I have opened up so much and have been able to express my opinions and ideas.

I also went to a meeting to talk to a group of professionals about the course to say how it had changed my life. I was nervous about it but I got up in front of 20 people and told them of my experience. It was one of the most scariest moments of my life but, it was also the most exciting and exhilarating thing I had ever done. After I finished I felt so great, I couldn't stop smiling and everyone was telling me how well I did. It was such an achievement I never would have done this if it wasn't for the course.

In the course, every week we were asked to do Success Diaries so that we all could recognise that we do have successes as parents no matter how little it is, it's still a success. This has helped a lot because I never thought I was good at anything and that whatever I did was a failure and to be honest it made me quite depressed but after doing the Success Diaries I realise I am not a failure and it makes me happy.

Another thing I learnt is, the art of meditation. I have heard about it before but wrote it off as a load of rubbish. I realise I should have been more open minded about it as it really does work. Before each session started the group closed their eyes and emptied their heads so that all the bad thoughts would leave our minds. I thoroughly enjoyed doing it because it made it easier to work and listen. Sometimes I found it hard but after practicing it at home it got easier and easier and now I feel confident enough to know I can do it.

This course has helped me in so many ways, it has made my life a lot easier and I'm a much happier person which makes my daughter happier too, which makes me happier and so the cycle keeps going.

I have met some fantastic people who I have become good friends with. We now meet up at each others houses to have a coffee and a chat.

If I hadn't been given the opportunity to be a part of the course then my life would still be the same as before and that's not a good thing. I also wouldn't have met the people I have
Ms K

(note: Ms K. you are the one that has done all the hard work to make these achievements possible, well done)

CHAPTER 8

Another resource

You gain strength, courage and confidence by every experience which you must stop and look fear in the face...You must do the thing you think you cannot do.
Eleanor Roosevelt

Imagine just how useful this resource anchor would be immediately before any situation that might otherwise be stressful. Creating a personal resource anchor provides a stimulus, which can be used as and when needed.

It is a reminder of when you were successful/confident/happy and can be drawn upon as and when the situation presents itself. It involves a simple procedure prompting a fast, intense sense of self-confidence and personal power.

You can read the script or it might be easier to have it read to you until you are familiar with it

1. Close your eyes and think about how you would feel if you could be successful or happy or confident etc at anything.

2. Think about a time you have been very successful/happy/ confident.

3. Float into yourself - see how you looked, hear how you sounded and feel how you felt.

4. Experience the brightness of the picture, the loudness of the sound and the intensity of those feelings.

5. Now double the brightness and double again. Hold that feeling and open your eyes.

6. Break your state (e.g. by remembering what you had for breakfast yesterday).

7. Now select a point on your body where you would like to have this anchor. This will be your anchor point. It might be the back of your hand on a knuckle, touching two fingers together or maybe on your ear lobe. Choose somewhere that is not likely to be touched by accident.

8. Touch your anchor point when you have created those intense feelings again.

9. Close your eyes once more and go back inside yourself to when you were successful/happy/confident and remember all those super sensations.

10. Think about how you looked, the sounds you heard and all those good feelings you had when you were successful/happy/confident.

11. Experience the brightness of the picture, the loudness of the sound and the intensity of those feelings.

---

12. Now double the brightness and double again and again.

13. At the peak of the intensity touch your anchor point.

14. Break your state (e.g. by remembering what you had for lunch yesterday).

15. Repeat the anchoring and breaking state several times until you feel that the emotion/feeling is well and truly anchored.

16. Now think of a time when you can use this situation in the future and feel the intensity of those experiences you have just had.

17. Test your anchor by touching the anchor point and noticing the effect. If you do not yet experience a strong sensation, repeat the process from step 9.

You can build on this anchor whenever you wish by touching your anchor point whenever you experience the same intense emotions/ feelings.

At last!

WOW this is the end of Part 1. I honour you for the commitment you have shown – congratulations and if you have time do drop me a line and let me know how your life is now, I would appreciate it.

Reference: This exercise comes from my Neuro Linguistic Programming training.

I'm confident you are a very different person now than when you first picked up the book. If you feel confident to work with your teen and they are ready – great. If not don't worry it will give you more time and opportunity to practice these new skills as they slowly become a part of your life.

Please remember you are changing the habits of a lifetime, so be gentle with yourself and don't beat yourself up if you drop back into old habits. The most wonderful thing to take away from this experience is you have tasted a different way to be with yourself, and you can choose when you want to change things again. You've done it once and the next time will be easier. Slowly you will realise the times between how you used to be and how you want to be, become less. New habits are formed and you are the different person you wanted to be!!!

Another change you might notice is some of the friends or acquaintance who might have taken advantage of your good nature, may fall away because you are not the easy touch you once were.

Sustainability

To ensure you really sustain your progress you may want to create your personal sustainability strategy for the future. Chapter 17 will give you lots of ideas on how to achieve that.

You are now ready to take the next step.

Case Study Mrs J

"Before the course when my eldest daughter (14 years old) approached me I might appear to be listening but not take on board what she was saying. I was also taking on the responsibility of everyone in the family which was giving me loads of stress and I never knew if I was coming or going.

The biggest thing I got from the course was the expansion exercise which gave me the power to realise I was in control of everything I do. I have now connected to my inner self giving me the ability to know what I need to do next.

The communication with my fellow buddies has allowed us to become an extended family, no matter what the challenge there is always someone to lend a helping hand. What we've realised is that we were always great but didn't know it.

'Level of listening' has helped me to listen to everyone on a much deeper level and everyone equally which has led to a remarkable change in atmosphere in the whole family. And the amount of arguments has reduced to only 25% of what they were and I can see that being reduced.

My eldest daughter was my biggest challenge but because of the work I have done on myself, she has responded with remarkable changes to her behaviour. I came to the course initially to help with these challenges and found it has impacted on every area of my life and our family.

My motto now is 'that anything is possible given the right resources'. I want to share the essence of what I have achieved with the world."
Mrs J

CHAPTER 9

A different approach

We are each of us angels with one wing.
And we can fly only by embracing each other.
Luciano de Crescenzo

We mentioned the coaching approach earlier in the book. Coaching is an internal process that enables a person to connect with their inner self and empowers them to make their own choices. Understanding and appreciating that we all have choices in life is a very powerful motivation.

The key to building a successful relationship is to see your children, particularly teenagers, in the same light as you see your best friend. Parents need to listen to their children's perspective, trust and respect them as individuals and support them through the issues that they are facing.

When parents or caregivers take this approach, incredible things happen to the relationship. After all, the stronger your relationship, the more influence you are likely to have. Unfortunately some parents believe they have control over their children when the most they have is influence. The more your children value the quality of the relationship the more influence they will have.

The coaching approach

One of the key tools a coach uses is the GROW model. GROW is an acronym for Goal, Reality, Options and When/Why. It's a simple tool will enable you to easily understand where your child is coming from and what is currently facing them.

The basis of this working relationship to create is as follows:

1. Respect each other and only one person talks at a time.

2. State that there are no wrong answers and that you are working to your child's agenda.

3. Make it clear that you will retain total confidentiality.

4. State that you are completely non-judgemental - and mean it.

5. Question incisively and listen very closely.

6. Do not put any of your ideas onto your child. You need to let them reveal what their chooses are. Your role is to delve deeper until it 'feels right'. The more options you help them explore the better.

7. It is vital that you give your child time to find the answers for themselves. The old 80/20 rule applies – 80% listening and 20% asking.

8. And most important make it fun for both of you.

Do not rush this process.

Here are some pointers to set the ball rolling, as you scan them a few will resonate and these will be the ones to focus on.

The GROW model

GOALS
1. How will you know when you have achieved your goal?

2. How will you hear, feel, show, when you have achieved your goal?

3. When do you want to be in this position? (The time-scale must be realistic). If the goal is big, break it down into smaller chunks.

REALITY
1. What is happening now and what is missing?

2. What is happening that is good and you want to keep?

3. What have you done and what were the results?

4. What is preventing you from moving forward?

5. What resources do you have and what do you need?

6. Review choice of issue/topic or make changes.

OPTIONS

1. What could you do to move yourself one step forward?

2. What would you be doing if:
   You were not answerable to anyone
   You had all the money in the world
   You could devote all your time to this

3. What could you do if you did not have to live with the consequences?

4. If you secretly knew what you should do first, what would it be?

5. Review options carefully - does this spark another idea?

6. Choose one option that will move you forward. It can be the easiest, cheapest or quickest.

7. Confirm that it will move you forward. What will the benefit be? Identify it and write it down.

WHEN/WHY

1. What are you going to do? What will you do? Will these actions meet your main goal?

2. When will you start? Should anyone else be involved? What will they do and when will you involve them?

3. Is there anything that could prevent this step from happening? How likely is it? How will you overcome it?

4. Earlier you wrote down your timescale. Is it still valid? Is there anything else you need to consider before you begin?

5. When will you actually start? Write the date in your diary, and ensure that you do.

I found the Options section the most powerful because it helped me break out of the circle of thoughts I was locked into.

Well done! You now have a better understanding of how the GROW model fits into the techniques of coaching.

It's now time to set up the Agreement.

Case Study Miss T

"After the first couple of weeks I realised I was very much there as a parent and not in a professional capacity. Although I have found the course has given me a great deal of confidence when dealing with parents at work. I have embraced the techniques to the best of my ability and found that they have made a considerable difference to my outlook of how I think about things generally and more specifically how I communicate with children, particularly my own.

I have passed on advice to parents about how to handle tricky situations with their children and also had a conversation with one about her low self esteem and how she doesn't give herself enough credit. I am encouraging parents to listen to their children at any opportunity I get and hear myself saying to people 'its about choice, you can choose....' I am in a great position within my job to 'spread the word' only last week at my coffee afternoon, I was talking to parents about taking responsibility and leading by example.

As a mum it has given me the opportunity to re connect with my son, who is 18 and having a very difficult time emotionally. I didn't think our relationship was too bad but I knew I found it hard to talk to him and understand what was going on in his head. Things are difficult still but we are talking more, he comes to me regularly to talk about what is on his mind and more recently he agreed to go and see a doctor which is something I have been asking him to consider for some time now. I also had my first real heart to heart with my 8 year old daughter last week. I know I am better able to listen now and give better responses and this is very much down to the course.

Finding my positive energy is something that I will choose to work at constantly, as I have seen definite improvements in my life and I appreciate that this is a small steps process but very much worth the effort."
Miss T

Reference: Sir John Whitmore introduced the GROW model and coaching into major multinationals in the UK over 30 years ago and today it's used in almost 90% of companies.

Sir John is now Chairman of our charity Every Family Matters.

CHAPTER 10

Setting up a Coaching Agreement

One of the most obvious facts about grown-ups, to a child, is that they have forgotten what it is like to be a child.
Randall Jerrell

If you want to create a structured approach with someone in your family, a working agreement provides a sound basis.

Explain that the concept of coaching is to empower individuals and share some of your experiences and successes you have achieved so far. If they would also like a different relationship, they have to be prepared to do something different to bring this about. In order to change things, you must both be committed to this agreement.

Don't force this step on your children if they are not ready. When I first stated this work it was with children and every single one I spoke to said one or more of the following. I'm not listened too. I'm not respected. I'm not valued. Until you have created an open communication this approach won't work.

Make a plan and schedule as though it was a formal course. Your child needs to know that this is going to be a new experience with different outcomes and it is based around what they want or need.

Discuss and agree the ideal time to start this activity and how long each session will last.

The age and level of development of your child will dictate the time span for which they will be at their most receptive. Once you have agreed on the schedule, you both need to ensure this time is kept sacrosanct. However, even though this is a formal agreement, you can still be light and happy and make it fun for both of you.

Don't forget to get into your most resourceful state before each session.

The Coaching Agreement

You can copy the following page, complete it and both sign it, even shake hands as well!

The
Coaching
Agreement

We the undersigned agree to work together for

_____ minutes, every _____ (day/days) to

create a different working relationship and based on

the coaching model a better outcome for the future.

Signed

_____ (coach)

_____ (coachee)

Date

_____

Case Study Mrs K

"My situation before this course was extremely confusing for myself and my children, it was very much dominated by fear and a lack of trust. It tore me and my kids apart that my kids heard and witnessed me being tormented, mentally, emotionally, sexually and physically as a way of coping day by day I shut down.

How could anyone hurt me so deeply again if I had no reaction, no emotion or feeling. Well that's what I would pretend and when I look back it was a survival instinct I developed to live. I wanted to move on so much but I no longer knew how to achieve it.

My children went from having a happy and secure life, to them living a living nightmare. Two of my children went within themselves no longer talking and sharing with me because they thought if they were really good the situation would go away. If a situation was a bad experience I would look at them and they would leave the room. The look was one of pleading, I don't want you to see, hear or feel this, although in my heart I knew they were very aware of the situation.

One of my kids would pretend it was not happening, he built up a fantasy which I had a hand in as not to shatter it, I blamed myself, made excuses. He went from a caring bright child that loved life and all in it, into a boy that hated me and he had a cynical approach to life, he cried in anger. My other two children shouted at me until they were blue in the face, on their hands and knees crying in physical and emotional pain, begging me to put things right again. All my children wanted was their Mum back, they cherished me as a Mum and believed I was a wonderful person in my own right and visa versa.

They didn't want the latest fashions, extra money or a Mum that did not have boundaries or discipline. My kids loved my honest approach towards them, the care, love, the way we had great fun. We all wanted our strong family to be again. With the course I and my kids have found a way that is working towards this. I don't expect things to go back to how they were before, as we have all changed and we are getting to know each other as the people we are now. But we all believe we will be stronger as a family and as individuals."

Mrs K

CHAPTER 11

Create the right environment

You don't have to be great to get going, but you have to get going to be great.
Les Brown

As your child looks on you as Mum, Dad or carer, and rightly accepts that home is full of love and lots of comforts, this may be a challenge. It may be difficult for them to accept you in the role of coach as they will more likely see you as a 'teacher' and may not want the feeling of being surrounded by 'learning and working'.

To help create this separation, work together in a study or spare room. If you can't provide a suitable room, consider creating a special area to work where you can create a different atmosphere.

Perhaps you can decorate it together with inspirational images and posters so that your child feels comfortable, happy and enjoys being there. Your interest, enthusiasm and desire will speak more loudly than the physical limitations you face and it will create a more effective result.

Remember - the more special they feel, the more successful you both will be. Let the child go at their own pace; there is no need to rush anything. Each child will work at a different speed and in a different way. Respect the individuality of your child. You might find it helpful to look at **Chapter 13 - Understanding how your child learns.**

Encourage your child to explore and expand their thoughts. Use metaphors in order to draw out the child's thoughts, prompting gently but being careful not to put words into his/her mouth. Metaphors are simple comparisons e.g. "as white as a sheet" or "as pretty as a picture".

You have now completed **Part 2 - When they are ready.** No doubt feeling excited by their involvement, it's time to go back to **Chapter 2 Getting in the mood** and starting to work through the exercises together. This is when you can share some of your learning and adapt the tools and techniques to suit them. Enjoy!!

Next is **Part 3 - Additional resources.** I wanted to give you other information parents have found useful as they work through the book.

Case Study Mrs J

"The reason I came to your group in the first place was that my daughter was being disruptive in school and at home. After working with you and then putting this into practice with her, it come to light that my daughter didn't like the person she had become, saying she was a nasty horrible person, but she didn't know how to move on from that.

I started by telling her that she has choices in life and we worked on from that. She made the most dramatic change within 3 weeks and went on to have a great summer. My daughter is now happy

---

and comfortable with herself and her teachers think she must have a twin!

By changing the way I think, having the time to listen and helping my daughter make the right choices has made our relationship much stronger. I know we only had 3 weeks together, but what I took away from that course was a whole new meaning to parenthood.

Putting it all into action with my children has made our lives as a family much closer. We all talk and listen to each other (most of the time)! I think for the children knowing that I'm on their side has been the biggest help for them, telling me things they never would have before, then us working it out together.

Life's not perfect all the time, but as long as we work this way, keeping it consistent, our relationship will be a good one. Due to all of this and because I've always had an interest, I am now doing a GCSE in Psychology. It was the push I needed. So many thanks' from a very content mother."
Mrs J

CHAPTER 12

A problem solving strategy

Although love is the most important requirement for parenting, it is not enough.
John Gray, 'Children are from Heaven'

Control your life! – it's an inside job

Inevitably there will be a clash of interests, ideas or views that lead to an argument. The following is a possible strategy to enable you to change the result from a downward spiral of aggravation, stress and confrontation to one of mutual understanding and respect.

Take time out

It's not easy in the heat of the moment to recognise what your thoughts are, so you need to take some time out to gather yourself. Take a deep breath and say 'I'm not in the right mood to talk about this now. Let's talk about it later'. You will notice that the shouting and arguing will stop as you are not responding and feeding the argument

Chill out

Use this lull in proceedings to gather yourself. Remember when you were in a very good mood or just feeling great. You need to recreate this 'feeling good' state. Think back to a time or situation when you were really, really happy. Remember how good you felt and what you heard, saw and felt then. Choose to hold these good feelings in your memory until you start to feel very good inside. Have you read **Chapter 4 – Another resource?**

It may not be easy right now but choose to and recall a situation when you felt love and/or respect for the person you are arguing with!

Separate the person from their behaviour

You may consider the behaviour of the other person is not acceptable, although the person is the same person whom you loved/respected at one time. We are all unique and special people who are reacting to our thoughts. The other person no doubt feels differently based on their thoughts!

It may be that they have just experienced a crisis in their life that you are not aware of. Equally, you may have been upset by something that happened to you earlier, something that has nothing to do with the person with whom you are now arguing.

So, two unrelated experiences create the frustration, anger and aggravation between you. However, it only needs one person to change this situation to produce a more satisfactory outcome.

Put the past behind you

However frustrating, upsetting or annoying it is, nothing can be done to change the past. You have to learn how to deal with it the best way you can to take the heat out of it - maybe talk to a good-friend or relative.

You have a choice here. You can either start to forgive and forget, or you can carry on letting the past have a negative impact on your life now and in the future.

Be curious

When you are feeling more forgiving, approach with respect and find out what is in the other person's life now and what concerns they have. When you have listened from your heart and understand exactly why they reacted as they did, you may want to explain where you were coming from and how you see things.

Be sure everything has been discussed and everything is out in the open.

Love and respect

Explain why you did not like their behaviour. Ask what it was about your behaviour that upset them and reassure them of your true feelings toward them. It may be that this was covered in the 'Be curious' step.

Tell the other person, but ONLY if you really mean it, you want to

re-establish your relationship/friendship as it was in the good times.

What can be done together?

Ask what can be done to overcome the argument. It may have to be a compromise for you but choose to, and accommodate as many as possible of the other person's ideas. It might even be that you need to do something that you are not happy to accept at first to ensure that the other person is in no doubt of your intention to listen to and act upon their ideas. You may want to create an Action Plan together.

When you are both relaxed, respected and feel listened to, each of you will be far happier with the other person.

Now you've learnt the principal tools and techniques that turned my life around and those of thousands of families who have followed them. The fantastic thing is that, the more congruent you are, the less you actually have to do in your own family because things change naturally around you

Case Study Mr D and Mrs A

It was Sunday 10th May, a beautiful sunny day and I was off to a Christening to celebrate the birth of baby J. It was no ordinary Christening and I was flattered to be asked to be a God Father. I will leave Mrs A to take up the story

"It was late June when I discovered I am pregnant again, I went to

see my doctor who said she would let the midwife know, and with that I went home and went onto the internet to look for parenting classes, I wanted to change things this time around. There were loads in Kent and 99% of them were free and I was looking down the list this one course jumped out at me. So I printed off the list and said no more, I gave it to D. He was going through it and the same one caught his eye, it was the only one you had to pay for so we picked that one and e-mailed the group straight away.

We got a call from a man called Alan Wilson he arranged to meet us at one of his Family Coaching Café taster sessions, we arrange to see him on 14th July at 2pm. We had a long chat and I explained our 6 children from previous marriages, were in care and why, he stopped us and said "to be honest as far as I'm concerned the past is the past and if you are both totally committed to a different future I can help you" – what a relief at last we had found someone who believes in us.

I went on to tell him the problems we were having with our eldest son, who is in a residential home. He looked at us and said "if you ask your son why he did what he did, he may not know why specifically and immediately be on the defensive. Try saying how can we support you to be better behaved, by asking him in this way he will be more likely give you a useful answer." I remember thinking to myself, yes whatever, you don't know him it's not that simple. When I spoke to him next I remembered what Alan had said so I tried it and it has worked his behaviour improved 100%.

L was a typical teenager who thought he knew everything, we applied some of the things we had talked about with Alan and helped him see things from different angles, for example, L was very hot headed which often ended up with a conflict of some sort with his peers in his care home. After listening to us he himself applied the skills we had learnt and to his surprise it worked, the conflicts were becoming fewer, his attitude has changed for the better and his language was far better then we could of dreamed of.

Over the weeks L had changed his behaviour beyond recognition, no more fighting with peers and staff, running away, stealing and being a constant worry. He has become a peer mentor to his colleagues and the staff cannot believe he is the same lad.

I believe if this approach can help L change then there is hope for other children and families out there. We see him as a typical teenager, who now, in his own mind is able to apply a positive thought process to many of things that he had struggled with, in fact he is starting to shine in many ways, for example, his school work had not been very good due to the conflict with his peers/ teachers, his general attitude to life since being placed into care was no one cared for him except us.

He started to apply some simple techniques that we had passed onto him which set him up to become a decent young man. His school work has improved, his school portfolio is so good he has obtained recommendation after recommendation and certificate after certificate, he is the only person in his year to complete it, all by just applying a positive mental attitude. L seemed keen to learn more because he was seeing the benefits that he had made himself. In fact he was so surprised by our changes he said on one occasion 'are you 2 on drugs, you have changed so much'.

If you are reading this and are in any doubt that this seems to good to be true, I challenge you the reader to put it to the test.

The rewards that can be generated by applying techniques that are so simple to master, are far greater then you can imagine. I urge you to think where you are in your life and where you want to be, because ultimately you make your own future and you have a choice at every event that plays a part in your life.

You need to be patient with yourself and follow your heart."
Mr D and Mrs A

CHAPTER 13

Understanding how your child learns

The single biggest problem in communication is the illusion that it has taken place.
George Bernard Shaw

The language you use with your child is extremely important. You are the role model and if you use inappropriate language he will too.

The following exercise will demonstrate the predominant method through which your child processes information and learns from it. When you present information in the way they processes it, their understanding will be clearer and the connection is deeper.

Children may struggle to choose between the four options. If this is the case, ask them to work with numbers 1 and 4 first, and then go back to 2 and 3. Do remember, there is no hurry to complete this exercise. The answers must come from your child and it might need a little thought. There are no wrong answers.

Depending on the level of development of your child, you may need to adapt the questions accordingly. Each question has a seeing, hearing, feeling and thinking answer. You can copy and complete the exercise on the following pages

---

'How children learn' exercise

For each of the statements, please place a number next to every phrase. Use the following system to indicate preferences.

4 = Closest to describing you
3 = Next best description
2 = Next best
1 = Least descriptive of you

1. I make important decisions based on:
* ____ gut feelings
* ____ which way sounds the best
* ____ what looks best to me
* ____ studying and thinking about the facts

2. During an argument, I am most likely to be affected by:
* ____ the other person's tone of voice
* ____ whether or not I can see the other person's point of view
* ____ the thought behind the other person's point of view
* ____ whether or not I care about the other person's feelings

3. Other people know what is going on with me by:
* ____ the way I dress and look
* ____ the feelings I share
* ____ the words I choose
* ____ the tone of my voice

Reference: adapted from Neuro Linguistic Programming Different Modalities

---

4. It is easiest for me to:
- ____ find the right radio station and volume on a stereo
- ____ select the most important point from an interesting subject
- ____ select the most comfortable furniture
- ____ select attractive colour combinations

5.
- ____ I am aware of the sounds of my surroundings
- ____ I am very capable of making sense of new facts and data
- ____ I am very sensitive to the way articles of clothing feel on my body
- ____ I react to colour schemes and to how a room looks

The Results of the Exercise

Step One

Copy your answers from the previous questions to the lines below.

1. ____ Feeling ____ Hearing ____ Seeing ____ Thinking

2. ____ Hearing ____ Seeing ____ Thinking ____ Feeling

3. ____ Seeing ____ Feeling ____ Thinking ____ Hearing

4. ____ Hearing ____ Thinking ____ Feeling ____ Seeing

5. ____ Hearing ____ Thinking ____ Feeling ____ Seeing

Step Two

Fill in the table below. Once the table is complete, add up all the numbers in each letter column to give a total for each letter.

	Seeing	Hearing	Thinking	Feeling
1				
2				
3				
4				
5				
Sub totals				
Totals	x2	combine hearing and thinking		x2

By doing this exercise I have discovered that my preferred way of learning is:_____

(the one that has the highest score)

This indicates the predominant way your child tends to process information. For example if their highest score was 'Seeing' you can ask 'how does this situation look to you?' If 'Hearing and Thinking' are the highest ask 'how does this situation sound to you?' Or if 'Feeling' was the highest, ask 'how does this situation feel for you?' The benefit of this exercise is that you will now know how to better communicate with your child.

Applications

The following characteristics will help you connect better with your children in everyday communication and support with their homework.

Seeing
- They use picture descriptions during conversation
- They are interested in how things look
- They must see things to understand them
- They like visually-based feedback

Communication and homework support can be more effective by working with references and resources featuring plenty of pictures.

Hearing and Thinking
- They can repeat things back easily
- They learn by listening
- They usually like music and talking on the phone
- They like to be told how they're doing

Communication and homework support can be more effective by reading to your child the homework material or reading in general and discussing the subject matter of references and resources.

Feeling
- They respond to physical rewards and touching
- They memorise by doing or walking through something
- They check out their feelings prior to expressing their thoughts
- They often move and talk slowly

Communication and homework support can be more effective by encouraging visualisation - doing/experiencing and feeling of the subject matter.

Remember that this exercise indicates the predominant method your child processes information - we all use all of the methods all of the time to a greater or lesser degree. However, people under stress usually revert to their predominant method.

Case Study Mrs B

"When I came to my first session, I can remember feeling quite low and not enjoying being a parent. I was feeling bored with life and felt that I needed something more to occupy my mind.

Although I have a very active 1 year old I was feeling like I wasn't achieving anything by looking after my daughter and thought that going back to work was the answer. Since then I have changed my outlook on life and how I see things at this point in my life and I believe this is down to your sessions.

I feel that by talking through what I have achieved in my life so far and by using the course materials to realise what I have, has made me realise that you don't need a lot to be really happy. I realised that being happy can affect so many different aspects of my life, such as my daughters moods and my relationship with my partner.

I know now that true happiness for me is being content with what I have got and what I have achieved already so far in my life, my daughter, my fiancé (we have got engaged since I have been attending your course), my house, etc.

Where as before, I felt like I needed to achieve more, I wasn't content with just being a mum and didn't see this as an important role. Now I embrace my role as a mother and enjoy each and every day with my daughter. I know these early stages in her life will go by so quickly, and as her mother I can offer her so much by being here at home with her.

I have also looked into and will be attending a seminar on becoming a life coach. You mentioned this to me after we did a session on what our real passions were, and from this I discovered that I enjoyed listening to people, helping and guiding people.

Thank you for all your guidance and support - it has changed my life"
Mrs B

CHAPTER 14

Connecting with your child

Our greatest glory is not in never falling, but in rising every time we fall.
Confucius – Philosopher

We've covered the 'energetic connection', fully in Chapter 5. This chapter is really old paradigm but it's still worth a read through, I particularly like the Use of Questions section.

The main areas are:
1. Respect
2. Levels of listening
3. Use of questions
4. Showing appreciation
5. Offering support

Respect

Apart from unconditional love and trust, respect is the most important characteristic or attribute we can have for another person. Look carefully at the following sentences and consider what impact on a relationship these would have if you were able to incorporate some

---

or all of them into your thinking and approach.

You know respect has to be earned and this exercise will give you some different perspectives on yourself and someone else you are in relationship with e.g. how a child, partner, colleague views their world.

1. Respect the other person's view of the world. It will help you connect with them and they will tend to respect you.

2. The response you get from someone is based on what they thought you meant, not from what you said. We are all different. We all understand things slightly differently and in our own unique way.

3. Your mind and body are connected. You cannot act happy if you are not feeling happy.

4. The words you use explain your perception of an event. The words themselves are not the reality. We can create more choices by changing our words.

5. You are doing the best you can with all the resources you have. Accept people are doing the best they can.

6. Accept the person as they are. Their behaviour is another issue.

7. You have all the resources you need to make the changes you want. If you are stressed you have the capability to change that emotion. You need to get in the right frame of mind to do something about it - something different from what you have been doing.

8. Possible in the world is also possible for me - it is only a matter of how you achieve it.

9. The more options you can create, the more choices you have.

10. There is no failure, only feedback. What have you learnt from trying something? All 'failures' are experiences. The more you try, the more successful you will become.

11. Everything you do should increase wholeness within you. Feel good about yourself, accept and respect other people as they are and be true to yourself.

Exercises

1. Choose the three sentences that resonate with you or that you really like the most.

2. Then put them in order with the most important as number 1.

3. Ask your child and/or partner to do the same.

4. Now compare.

This exercise underlines the fact that we all perceive life from different perspectives. The more you respect other people's model of the world, the more they will respect you. You will also have a deeper connection with that person.

Is the situation right to ask your child if they feel respected by you? If not, what can you do for them to feel respected by you?

And, whom don't they feel respected by? What does that person need to do for them to feel respected?

Levels of Listening

When I first did my coach training I thought 'active listening' was the most sensitive form of listening. These are the levels of listening, as I now understand them.

1. No listening - pretty obvious really. They are day-dreaming or looking out the window.

2. Listening to the words - they are looking and apparently listening, but you can tell it's not going in.

3. Listening beyond the words - really thinking about what is being said, communicated or meant.

4. Active listening - this was the most powerful level of listening when I first took my coach training. It's all your receptors on high alert, like your best friend is going to tell you something no one else knows. Open body language, eyes glistening and very keen to know what's going on..

5. Energetic listening/connection - see Chapter 5

Qualities of a good listener

a) Genuine Interest

When we listen to a child, we need to demonstrate that they really are important. A good listener shows that they are really interested, really care and are really committed to what the child is sharing with us. It never ceases to amaze me how much wisdom there is in a very young child – we need to help them explore their feelings and ideas

b) Respect

Listen with respect to what your child has to say. It may be rather boring, or you may have heard it before but remember he is demonstrating his respect for you by wanting to share his information with you. He will be delighted and empowered if you listen with interest. He may contradict what you know or believe to be true but whatever is said by him at that moment is important and true for him. It is how he sees it.

Communication should be mutually beneficial, meaning your child should equally learn to listen to your point of view. Each of you is entitled to expect respect.

c) Empathy

Listening from the child's perspective, rather than your own, enables you to see the world through his eyes. This means you can 'feel with' your child, rather than 'feel like him'. When your child knows that you understand at this level, he is much more likely to continue the communication and be willing to express emotions that may be uncomfortable for him and be open to moving the subject on.

When you hear something you don't want to hear – take a deep breath and think, 'will what I am about to say move me nearer or further away from my child?' Remember, the better the relationship you have, the more influence you will have.

d) Clarity

Your child may express all sorts of vague notions and ideas. He may come to you not knowing what he really wants or what he needs to do. As a good listener you will be able to clarify his vague and muddled ideas by helping him to be more specific, by exploring what he is trying to convey to you, by asking lots of open questions (see two pages further on) and listening to his answers. Remember to avoid rushing him and allow time for him to process a considered answer. Also don't assume you know the answer; this will dull your deeper listening skills.

e) Articulation

As a good listener, you will be able to reflect back the essence of what your child has said, succinctly describing the situation. This often helps him to see the situation more clearly or differently. Good articulation is a way of demonstrating that you have heard and under-stood what has been said. It grows the confidence of your child because he knows you are listening, have heard what he has said, have empathy with his feelings and respect for what he is saying.

f) Immediacy

You need to understand the dynamics of the conversation, how to know when to ask your child another question or not; how to sense that you are going round in circles and when to clarify. Immediacy is a continuous awareness of what is happening in the conversation. It is interpreting those hidden messages portrayed by tone, facial expression and body language.

Use of Questions

You may be alarmed at the thought of questioning your child; it sounds rather intimidating. See the use of questions in a different frame, one in which you are seeking to find out your child's:

- Point of view
- Perspective
- Ideas
- Feelings
- Wants
- Needs
- Aspirations

Asking questions reflects your interest, your desire to build rapport and connect with your child. Remember when your child was about 2 and he constantly asked 'why?' and how you would consistently respond wanting to satisfy his thirst for knowledge.

It's now your turn for a real thirst for knowledge for what your child thinks and feels about specific situations or just life in general.

Questions are the key to engaging and connecting with your child. The types of questions you use are vital. And this is the time to use open questions. I think it is vital to spend time clarifying what these are and to consider the effect they and other types of questions have when engaging in conversation with our children.

Open questions are questions fronted with, What – When – Where – Who and How. I have left out Why because its impact can be confrontational. '**Why did you do that?**' is far more intrusive and provocative than, '**What made you do that?**' which seeks the same answer, yet it is softer and more encouraging.

All the words mentioned require a fuller answer than 'yes' or 'no'. If the question can be answered with a brief 'yes' or 'no' it is a closed question.

Example using a leading/closed question

'**Did you play football today?**' leads your child to say, '**Of course I did**', or a simple '**Yes**', cutting down the opportunity to engage in warm and genuine engagement. '**A good game was it?**' leads him to think the answer you want is '**yes, it was a good game**' and so he responds accordingly.

Now try with an open question:

'**How did the football game go today**?' This question shows a real interest and requires a fuller response to your question which can lead to the use of further open questions, such as,

'Who did you play against?'
'Where was the match played?'
'When's the return going to be?'
'What do you think the team needs to do, to improve/build on today's success?'

There is, of course, an implied expectation here that the game could have been improved or that there is room to build on today's success. Be careful not to imply that you think that his performance wasn't good enough.

Homework is a subject that is often a matter of contention. Apply a Leading Question and you shut down avenues of communication. 'Did you do your homework after you came in from school?' leads your child to say, 'Of course I did', or a simple 'Yes'.

Try that with an Open Question:

'What homework did you have this evening?' Your child has got to think now and phrase an answer that requires some detail. You can of course follow it with other open questions to further demonstrate your interest.

'When has it got to be in by?'
'How do you feel about what you have done?'
'Where did you find out the information to write the essay?'
'Who would be the best person to help you with that?'

Closed Questions

Remember a closed question is one that your child can answer with a yes or no. If you want more than a yes or no answer, ask an open question. There is a place for closed questions. For example, if you want to know the answer to a simple question or if you want a direct answer to something specific, such as: **'Did you and your friends eat the packet of cakes in the cupboard which were for your brother's birthday party?'**

You may want to follow it up with some open questions to find out more, such as: **'What made you do it?'** **'How can you atone for it?'** **'When will you buy another packet?'** **'Who are you going to apologise to?'**

Multiple Questions

You will often hear TV interviewers asking multiple questions. The person being asked doesn't know which question to answer first or he conveniently 'forgets' the part of the question he does not want to answer.

Keep your questions simple, one at a time and open.

Powerful Questions

Powerful questions can help your child to make a quantum leap in perception or understanding, for example: **'What do you really want?'** invites introspection and soul searching. **'How will you know?'** asks your child to look into the future.

Perhaps the best question is **'What is the potential of this situation?'**.

'Where will this lead?' **'What is stopping you?'** **'What is the truth?'**

are all powerful questions. If he wants to do something, ask him on what basis he is making his decision.

Probing Questions

Probing questions may be required to seek out hidden factors. They may be hidden intentionally or unintentionally. Probing questions do not need to be harsh or intimidating: they can be used gently and sensitively. One of my favourite questions in reply to the famous 'I don't know' answers, is **'Well, if you did know what would it be?'** This encourages the child to go deeper.

Your child may be frightened or distressed, or possibly just unwilling, for all sorts of reasons, to be honest about a subject. This is when immediacy in your listening is all-important.

Remember:

You need to understand the dynamics of the conversation, how to know when to ask your child another question or not; how to sense that you are going round in circles and when to clarify.

Immediacy is a continuous awareness of what is happening in the conversation. It is interpreting those hidden messages portrayed by tone, facial expression and body language. It helps if you're calm and objective to get into this deeper listening state.

It is really important that children learn to ask their own questions and equally important to be given proper answers.

Showing appreciation

It may seem obvious that showing appreciation of our children is important.

However, how often do you do it? Appreciation is sharing pleasure in an achievement or showing understanding of how difficult something is for them.

Remember when listening with empathy, you're listening from the child's perspective rather than your own. This enables you to see the world through your child's eyes. It means you can 'feel with' your child, rather than 'feel like' your child.

Here are a few examples of appreciation to prompt you to think about how you could express your appreciation of your child even further and make a greater impact on both your lives.

'I appreciate that this situation has been very difficult for you and you have found it very uncomfortable to tell the truth because it meant involving your friends. I think you have been very strong, and have come to the right decision.'

'I really appreciate your clearing the table for me. It means so much to me when I don't have to keep asking you to do your share of the chores.'

'I really appreciate you don't like doing your homework. However, what do you think is in it for you?'

Don't be afraid to ask your child to explain how to programme the video recorder or DVD, i.e. something he is really good at.

It is also very empowering for a child when you admit making a mistake to them.

There are of course the wonderful times when you can just say, 'well done'/'what a wonderful drawing'/'thank you'/'I love you'. The question is - can you do more of it?

It may be fun to use the exercise you completed at the beginning of the book with your child to explore what he thinks he is good at and what he thinks is good in his life right now. This will give you a perspective on how your child sees himself and will enable you to add to the lists of what you think he is good at and what is good in his life.

It would also be fun to ask him what he thinks you are good at and what is good in your life. This would give a wonderful insight into how he sees you and the way you live your life. The next step would be to explore what your child thinks he is not good at and what is not good in his life.

You could then spend time with him exploring what opportunities there are to change these things and develop a plan to make it happen. Are you ready to ask what your child thinks you are bad at and what he thinks is not so good in your life at the moment?

In terms of appreciation, always show and tell your child you love him, and give him plenty of hugs and affection. Your child wants attention and compliments without strings attached, or as bait for something you want done or as evidence of what a good parent you are. Be there for them.

When giving a compliment, link it to a value or attribute. For example, 'I really respect your persistence in completing that challenge'. This can help overcome the 'false' self-esteem, created by showering compliments and appreciation on small or minor endeavours. When you encourage him to explore his own ideas and to find his own solutions, rather than you providing him with all the answers, your child's self-esteem will increase naturally.

It is valuable to realise that only you can change yourself or your view of someone else.

Remember, everyone's perception is different and everyone is different.

Offering Support

In part, this will be achieved by changing your role to that of a coach, a parent who is connected to his child's aspirations/wants/needs / concerns/challenges. You are working toward his self-empowerment.

Allow your child to experiment (within reason) to build his confidence and trust in himself. Make it fun. Encourage him to balance your housekeeping, change the oil in the car or change a plug, help you with some cooking or the washing-up. Allowing him to become involved in this way will create momentum and foster in him a sense of responsibility. It is very important to stress that mistakes are an opportunity to learn.

We can all reflect on times in our life when we have been told not to do something, or of its likely negative outcome, and have done it anyway. We have had to learn for ourselves. So it is with children. The skill is in not making the same mistake twice!

This is an important area where your child requires support, enabling him to learn from an outcome that has led to difficulties. Be there for him, help him to learn from it and encourage him to pick himself up and start again.

Of course, he can equally learn from success.

Look for the behaviour you want to acknowledge, build on it and develop it. Comment on it positively and ask open questions to explore how your child feels about it and what the benefits are (what's in it for them). Encourage your child to dream and to have goals to which he can aspire.

Encourage him to keep a journal of all the things he does, noting those he is proud of and acknowledging those he is not and record what he has learnt from the experience.

As your child seeks independence, respect his privacy and give him time for studies, jobs and extracurricular activities. Celebrating success and reflecting on his achievement is an essential ingredient in supporting your child.

Try not to make celebrating success a sequence of material rewards. Praise and appreciation can be far more effective. Connecting with your child is being there for him, being willing to learn and grow together, and rejoicing in all that you do together.

Case Study Mrs S

"Before I started the course all my children were suffering due to B's behaviour. L was going into herself and J was becoming a handful again. I was suffering as I felt as if I was a failure as a parent.

I involved Social Services because I felt as though I could not cope with all the problems he was having. There was no mutual respect between us and this made me worse in the way I was feeling and thinking. Most of the time I would let the kids walk all over me and get away with it.

Since starting the course the positive mental attitude I have found has made life better for all of us. I have found that changing the way I think has changed the way I talk to the children. There is not any more screaming or shouting above them. We now choose to and talk to each other. Not always possible but we are getting there.

As a family we also do more together, it is not me and my husband or them, it is us as a family. There is more respect between us all and even my husband has settled down and backs me up when I do have to tell them off for bad behaviour.

I now enjoy being a parent and spending the time doing things as a family. Also since the positive attitude has had a major effect on the forthcoming birth of our forth child. When the children were first told about the baby it was mine and his as time has gone by it has become ours and if you ask any of the kids who ours is they will go through the whole family by name.

With the whole family getting on better I do not feel a failure. I enjoy being a Mum."

Mrs S

CHAPTER 15

Some exercises for the younger person

Self esteem happens after action, not before
Olivia Landsberg

The Power of thought

You may want to use or adapt some of the tools that have been successful for you in the foregoing pages. I've adapted the 'Power of thought' for younger children in the creation of a Happy Book.

Create the Happy Book together and, as you do, tell the story of how they can use the book. Perhaps, when they are not so happy, they can go somewhere quiet with their Happy Book and, by working through the book, they will be able to be happy again.

Explain how, if they choose to think happy thoughts, they will slowly start to feel a little happier. As that feeling grows, if they concentrate hard on their happy thoughts, they will start to really BE happy again.

See the plan and example for content

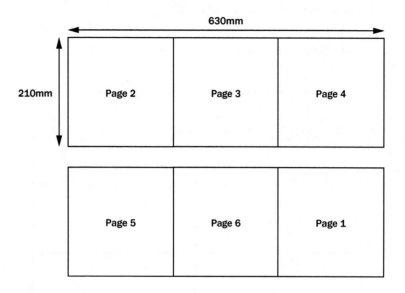

Page 1 **My Happy Book by** (name) (- their own personal copy)

Page 2 **I can choose to:** (it is their choice of how they feel)

- Think happy
- Feel happy
- And be HAPPY

Page 3 **My happy face** (a picture of themselves)

Page 4 **My sad face** (it is unfortunate, but there are times when we do feel unhappy - life happens)

Page 5 **What makes me feel HAPPY** (in a think bubble put pictures of all the special things that REALLY MAKE THEM FEEL HAPPY)

Page 6 **I AM HAPPY!** (feel wonderful in all their whole body or keep working through the book until they do)

Example - My Happy Book

PAGE 1	PAGE 2
My Happy Book by Cassy Wilson	I am cross to: Think happy Feel happy And be HAPPY!

PAGE 3	PAGE 4
My happy face	My sad face

PAGE 5	PAGE 6
What makes me feel HAPPY!	I AM HAPPY!

As you work through the book, show the main pages 2 and 5 together, the statement of choice and how important the 'thought' is to the whole story. Show how reading through from page 1 to page 6 shows and tells the whole story.

I hope you enjoy this special time with your child.

NB.   Even though this application is specifically for children, the overriding strategy works for everyone.

Values and positive affirmations

1. Elicit some values your child is proud of, for example, 'Toby said I am very clever'.

2. Create positive affirmations from these values. Each morning get your child to stand in front of a mirror and repeat three times 'I am very clever'. Another very powerful affirmation is 'I like myself'. Or you can create a positive affirmation from something your child is particularly proud of from the 'I am special' exercise on the following pages.

To make positive affirmations effective, they must be believable to our conscious minds before they are accepted by our subconscious minds:

1. It must be personal and start with 'I am' or 'I can'

2. Word it as though you already have made the change you want to make and use the present tense.

3. Visualise yourself achieving your desired outcome in a large colourful picture.

4. Be specific about the result of your affirmation.

5. Inject feeling and emotion into your affirmation. The change won't happen if you don't believe it will.

6. Affirmations are more effective if said when you are in a relaxed state, either when you wake up or just before going to sleep.

7. Repetition is the key but remember to add feeling and emotion each time you make an affirmation.

I am special

Have fun and create an 'I am special' worksheet (or copy the following page) and include:

Something I do to help my family is:
Something I do to help my teacher is:
Something I can do well is:
Something I am happy about is:
Something I wish I could do better is:
Something I like about the way I treat others is:
Something I like about myself is:

Also make a box for his thumbprint, signature or picture of himself.

Worksheet - I am special

Something I do to help my family is:

_____

_____

_____

_____

_____

_____

_____

Something I do to help my teacher is:

_____

_____

_____

_____

_____

_____

_____

Something I can do well is:

_____

_____

_____

_____

_____

_____

_____

Something I am happy about is:

_____
_____
_____
_____
_____
_____
_____
_____
_____

Something I wish I could do better is:

_____
_____
_____
_____
_____
_____
_____
_____

Something I like about the way I treat others is:

_____
_____
_____
_____
_____
_____
_____
_____

Something I like about myself is:

_____

_____

_____

_____

_____

_____

_____

_____

_____

My thumbprint/signature/photo

Journal or diary

Encourage your child to keep a journal or a Success Diary of all the things he does well. This will reinforce his learning and provide a great opportunity for him to look back and see how far he has come.

Case Study Mrs KC

What was my life like before the course?

I react to situations very quickly and emotionally and feel like I am living on my nerves. I look at things from a negative point of view and always feel like people are judging me, especially as a parent. I find it hard to take any advice on board and tend to take any suggestions as criticism. I find it hard to cope when my son isn't doing as I would like him to do and tend to shout at him in these situations. I find it hard to relax. I feel lonely, lost and have little confidence in myself.

What are the problems and issues?

I am not enjoying motherhood as much as I would like to. I find it hard to control my temper. I feel negative and useless. Relationships are suffering because of this particularly with my husband, son and mum.

What did I take from the course?

The course gave me the time and opportunity to find myself as a person again and to look closely at why I was reacting to situations as I was. I have realised that I need to love myself and that I have all the answers within myself and that I shouldn't look to others to solve my problems for me.

What really worked for me and my family?

I found the success diaries really useful. They helped me to focus on the positives and not dwell on the negatives and to realise that even on the worst of days there was some good.

I found the Wheel of Life particularly useful in realising that I haven't focused on myself as a person for such a long time and that really I had forgotten my own dreams.

Setting myself realistic goals gives me a sense of purpose and achievement.

What is my life like now I've completed the course?

I feel like I am finding the old me again. I am more relaxed and happy and as such my relationship has improved with both my child and my husband. By listening to my son more and understanding where he is coming from we clash much less and are both much happier and more relaxed.

Words can't really do justice to how far I feel I've come as a person since doing the course, I just feel so much more positive inside.

I am on a journey of self discovery.

What successes have I achieved?

I listen to my son more and feel more connected to him and his needs.

I trust my own instincts and believe in myself

I am more positive and make the decision not to dwell on negative thoughts and to replace them with positive ones

I am less judgemental of others

I put myself in a resourceful state and think situations through rather than react emotionally or lose my temper

I am happier inside

I am learning to love myself!
Mrs KC

CHAPTER 16

Celebrate each and every step

Concentrate on what you want, not on what you fear.
(Based on the Law of Attraction).
Tony Robbins

Celebrating success is critical. Celebrating can be anything from spending some extra time doing something your child likes and reflecting on his achievement, to sharing his progress with a special friend. Be creative.

Avoid material rewards and again, remember - there is no such thing as failure. If your child does not achieve what he sets out to do right away, it is important to know why and they must not feel a failure. Explain that even though he does not achieve his goal this time, he has already achieved a great deal: looking back over the exercises will reinforce this.

If desirable, you can gently look at some possible reasons including:

1. What is holding you back from achieving your goal?
2. How important is the goal for you right now?
3. What needs to happen so that you can achieve your goal?
4. How is not achieving your goal affecting you?

It is vital to celebrate the successful achievement of a goal and to ask your child how he felt in achieving it. (NB: The longer you can make this good feeling last, the more likely he will progress and achieve future goals more easily.) See Chapter 8 for anchoring a resource.

Case Study Mrs S

"From walking into the family room on the first week of this course not knowing what to expect, I am now on week five and feel really good about myself. Not having any behaviour problems with my son, I went in with a completely open mind and I am very glad that I did. I am open to all suggestions.

The way the trainer teaches a group is excellent. He doesn't preach to you but explains everything to you for you to digest as you will. There is no right or wrong answer, he introduces different ways of handling different situations. The major thing that I have learnt from this course is the power of thought. It is true what they say, 'Children can tell what mood you are in'. By changing the way you think and feel about yourself lets you change the way people react to you. By not shouting at people when you are cross makes them react different.

I really enjoy the group discussions in this class and the way he makes you feel really good about yourself. I am a very confident person anyway, but most of the group are not. By this short length of time in his class he has made the rest of the group change the way they think and become more positive.

I have learnt how to take control of my life and make more time for myself. This was one of my problems to start with as I had very little time to relax. I have managed to fit in time for myself and time for my family etc. In heated moments, I now don't just shout and argue, I say 'I'm not in the right mood to talk about this now, let's talk later. More often than not now, I have a cup of tea etc and then the relevant person comes and explains themselves and apologises. The stress is gone which is good. I have also learnt not to say just no but to explain to my son or whoever exactly why he or I can't do something and arrange when we can.

Another major thing I have learnt is to only say yes to something if I can give 100% to the project. By keeping a success diary, I found that I could record all my feelings and emotions that I felt in the course of a week and could clearly see all my successes and achievements. From these successes, clear goals could then be set and progress can be made. I found the levels of listening very interesting as it made me think hard about what you do when you are with other people, I am now able to listen properly and digest what people are saying.

The exercise we did on telepathy particularly interested me. Both myself and my partner quite often know what each other is thinking about. To some people it is very strange and not natural, but it was proved last week that it does work. The trainer speaks about sixth sense as well. I am a great believer in this as I am very interested in the new age ideas that he has.

It has been a great pleasure in doing this course. Currently, I am in the process of making a SMART goal and look forward to achieving it. I would recommend this course to everybody as if you are not confident to begin with, you will be by the end of this course.

After doing this course, it has left me hungry to find out more information about life coaching etc. One day I may become one myself as it interests me so much. This has been brought forward by just four weeks of a six week course. If I had been on a longer course, then who knows where I would end up!"

Mrs S

CHAPTER 17

Review and sustainability

Love is what we are born with. Fear is what we learn. The spiritual journey is the unlearning of fear and prejudices and the acceptance of love back in our hearts.
Love is the essential reality and our purpose on earth. To be consciously aware of it, to experience love in ourselves and others, is the meaning of life.
Meaning does not lie in things.
Meaning lies in us.
Marianne Williamson on Love (from 'Return to Love')

Finally it would be fun to see how far each of you has come. Copy and complete the following review forms separately and then share what you have learnt and experienced.

Name (child): _____ Date _____:

When we started, what did you hope to get from this activity?

_____
_____
_____
_____
_____
_____
_____
_____

I wanted to achieve because:

_____
_____
_____
_____
_____
_____
_____

Now we have finished, I feel I have gained/achieved:

_____
_____
_____
_____
_____
_____
_____

I ~~DON'T~~ KNOW YOU ~~ANY~~MORE

_____

Now we have finished, I feel I have not gained/achieved:

_____

_____

_____

_____

_____

_____

_____

_____

The thing(s) I plan to use now is/are:

1. _____

_____

_____

_____

_____

_____

_____

2. _____

_____

_____

_____

_____

_____

_____

_____

3. _____

_____

_____

_____

_____

_____

_____

_____

I would now like to achieve and will

_____

_____

_____

_____

_____

_____

_____

_____

_____

Name(parent): _____ Date _____

When we started, what did you hope to get from this activity?

_____
_____
_____
_____
_____
_____
_____
_____

I wanted to achieve because:

_____
_____
_____
_____
_____
_____
_____
_____

Now we have finished, I feel I have gained/achieved:

_____
_____
_____
_____
_____
_____
_____
_____

_____

_____

_____

Now we have finished, I feel I have not gained/achieved:

_____

_____

_____

_____

_____

_____

_____

The thing(s) I plan to use now is/are::

1. _____

_____

_____

_____

_____

_____

_____

2. _____

_____

_____

_____

_____

_____

_____

3. _____

_____

_____

_____

_____

_____

_____

_____

I would now like to achieve and will

_____

_____

_____

_____

_____

_____

_____

_____

Sustainability

In a workshop setting a powerful and moving exercise is a peer review. Each person says what they most respect of his or her fellow participants. This is recorded and circulated afterwards, I have seen grown men cry during these sharings. This exercise is not so easily replicated unless you have a group of family members all participating in a programme.

Another exercise in the final session of a course is where participants record the exercises that has had the biggest impact on them during the course. They then commit to doing one of them regularly. The winners are usually the success diaries completed by each member of the family and shared at a group meeting every week. Or, for individuals, practicing the 'energetic connection'.

Your children...

Your children are not your children.
They are sons and daughters of life's longing for itself.
They come through you but not from you,
And though they are with you, yet they belong not to you.
You may give them your love but not your thoughts
For they have their own thoughts.
You may house their bodies but not their souls,
For their souls dwell in the house of tomorrow, which you cannot
visit, not even in your dreams.
You may strive to be like them, but seek not to make them like you.
For life goes not backward nor tarries with yesterday.
Kahlil Gibran (1883-1935)

Note from the Author

Congratulations! You will have changed your life and developed your child into a more empowered individual who will go forward and be more successful.

Good luck in all you are doing to develop your child.
Alan Wilson

For more information and free resources visit:

www.developyourchild.co.uk

and

www.everyfamilymatters.org.uk

PS   If you have enjoyed using this book, please tell your friends. If you haven't, please tell me.

Bibliography

Books

A New Earth – awakening to your life's purpose by Eckhart Tolle published by Plume. ISBN 978-0-452-28996-3

Awesomism! A new way to understand the diagnosis of autism by Suzy Miller published by iUniverse. ISBN 978-1-4401-0285-1

Best Practice in Performance Coaching by Carol Wilson published by Kogan Page. ISBN 978-0-7494-5082-3

Be The Change by Trenna Cormack published by Love Books. ISBN 978-0-9555213-0-0

Choice Theory by William Glasser, published by Harper Perennial. ISBN 0-06-093014-4

CLICK by Ori Brafman and Rom Brafman published by Virgin Books. ISBN 978-0-7535-39-39-2

Coaching Evoking Excellence in Others by James Flaherty, published by Butterworth Heinemann. ISBN 0-7506-9903-5

Coaching for Performance by John Whitmore, published by Nicholas Brealey. ISBN 1 85788 303-9

Coaching in Education Edited by Christian van Nieuwerburgh published by Karnac Books Ltd ISBN 9 781780 49-793

I ~~DON'T~~ KNOW YOU ~~ANY~~MORE

Coaching With Spirit by Ter-E Belf published by Jossey-Bass/Pfeiffer. ISBN 0-7879-6048-9

Co-Active Coaching by Laura Whitworth, Henry Kimsey-House and Phil Sandahl, published by Davies-Back Publishing. ISBN 0-89106-123-1

Depressive Illness – the curse of the strong by Dr Tim Cantopher published by Sheldon Press ISBN 978 1 84709 235 9

Developing Intuition by Shakti Gawain published by New World Library. ISBN 1-57731-186-8

For Parents and Teenagers : Dissolving the Barrier Between You and Your Teen by William Glasser, published by Harper Collins Publishers. ISBN 0-06-000799-0

Getting Into The Vortex by Esther and Jerry Hicks published by Hay House USA. ISBN 978-1-4019-3169-8

Helping Kids Help Themselves by E Perry Good published by New View Publications. ISBN 0-944337-08-2

How to Help Children Find The Champion Within Themselves by David Hemery published by BBC Worldwide Ltd. ISBN 0-563-51968-1

How to Talk so Kids Can Learn at Home and in School by Adele Faber and Elaine Mazlish published by Piccadilly Press. ISBN 1-85340-704-6

It's Not How Good You Are, It's How Good You Want To Be by Paul Arden published by Phaidon Press Ltd. ISBN 978-0-7148-4337-7

Leadership Book for Youth, Parents and Teachers by Sai Baba published by Sri Sathya Sai Books. ISBN 81-7208-444-7

Life Force: The Scientific Basis by Dr Claude Swanson published by Poseidia Press ISBN 978-0974526140

Messages from Water by Masaru Emoto published by Hado Publishing BV. ISBN 908074213-9

Notes from a Friend by Anthony Robbins published by Pocket Books. ISBN 0-7434-0937-X

NLP at Work by Sue Knight published by Nicholas Brealey. ISBN 1 85788 302-0

Paranoid Parenting by Frank Furedi published by Continuum. ISBN 978-1-84706-521-6

Parent as Coach by Diana Haskins. published by Hara Publishing Group. ISBN 1-883697-77-8

Practising the Power of NOW by Eckhart Tolle published by Hodder and Stoughton. ISBN 0-340-82253-8

Psych-K The Missing Piece Peace in Your Life by Robert M. Williams, MA published by Myrddin Publishing. ISBN 0-759354-0-2

Serendipity's Secret by Samantha Babbington published by The Book Guild Ltd. ISBN 978-1-84624-456-8

Social Intelligence – the new science of human relationships by Daniel Goleman published by Arrow Books. 978-0099-46492-1

Supercoherence by Thrity Engiineer published by Hay House ISBN 978-1-4019-1584

Synchronicity The Inner Path of Leadership by Joseph Jaworski published by Berrett-Koehler Publishers, Inc. ISBN 978-1-60994-017-1

TA Today by Ian Stuart and Vann Joines published by Russell Press Ltd. ISBN 1-870244-00-1

The 10-Minute Life Coach by Fiona Harrold published by Hodder and Stoughton. ISBN-0-340 82201-5

The Alchemical Coach by Soleira Green published by Pinestream Publishing. ISBN 91-85393-07-X

The Bond by Lynne McTaggart published by Hay House UK Ltd. ISBN 978-1-84850-478 -

The Family Coach Method by Dr Lynne Kenny published by St Lynn's Press. ISBN 978-0-9819615-0-7

The Healing Code by Alexander Loyd and Ben Johnson published by Hodder & Stoughton. ISBN 978-1-444-72771-5

The Naked Leader by David Taylor published by Bantam Books. ISBN 0-553-81565-2

The New Psycho-Cybernetics by Maxwell Maltz, published by Souvenir Press. ISBN 0-285-63657-X

The Purpose of Your Life by Carol Adrienne published by Thorsons. ISBN 0-7225-3727-1

The Sixth Sense of Children : Nurturing Your Child's Intuitive Abilities by Litany Burns published by New American Library. ISBN 0-451-20525-1

The Tipping Point by Malcolm Gladwell published by Abacus. ISBN 0-349-11346-7

Time to Think by Nancy Kline published by Ward Lock. ISBN 978-0-7063-7745-3

Transform Your Life by Penny Ferguson published by The Infinite Ideas Company Ltd. ISBN 978-1-904902-65-2

Uncommon Sense for Parents With Teenagers by Michael Riera, published by Celestial Arts. ISBN 0-89087-749-1

Who Am I? Why Am I Here? by Patricia Diane Cota-Robles published by New Age Study of Humanity's Purpose. ISBN 978-0-9823260-1-5

Your Child by American Academy of Child Adolescent Psychiatry, published by Harper Resource. ISBN 0-06-273730-9

Videos

The Secret (2006) Sophie Angelle, John Assaraf, Anthony Baron, et al. ASIN: B000KK22GU

What the Bleep do we know? (2005) Marlee Matlin, Elaine Hendrix, and John Ross Bowie. ASIN: B0009S4W5C

No arms No legs No worries Nick Vujicic (2009) Nick Vujicic ASIN: 7561327102

About the Author

Alan began his career in the advertising and marketing industry over thirty years ago and has a proven track record of achievement, developing a successful group of creative production companies. His ethos was to challenge and support his clients to create a differential from their competitors. A marketing strategy was created to promote their unique solution, which invariably led to satisfied and profitable clients despite their competitive environments.

Going inward and making a difference

He became frustrated with a lack of new challenges and began to look for something more meaningful. Alan underwent a period of self-examination and reflection and investigated many complementary therapies. He came to the conclusion that, in order to fulfil his purpose, he needed to pursue a career where he could make a real difference to other people and, in particular, to the lives of children.

Alan has been married twice and has three children, Toby - 35, Holly - 33 and Cassy - 21. When Cassy was born, he realised he needed to reassess his parenting skills. He also recognised that his perspective of children related to his business philosophy i.e. find your good points and then build on them. It seemed a logical progression to marry that philosophy with his business acumen to set about making a positive impact on people's lives - but how?

Humbled, moving forward

Following a meeting with a Life Coach, this idea became a serious goal for him - to find a way to help people to achieve their potential. His own life coaching training followed and he describes this experience as 'humbling and exciting'. To further enhance his skills in enabling others to become self-empowered, he has trained in parent coaching, Neuro-Linguistic Programming (NLP) and complementary therapies. Alan is now committed to a life-long quest of personal development and growth.

Eureka!

Realising that these techniques could be adapted for children, Alan approached the Head Teacher of his children's school and together they developed a pilot scheme to help the children become more confident, more fulfilled and better learners. His target group of eight-year-olds responded well but, although the project was reasonably successful, it was far from perfect. A similar project, this time targeted at teenagers, was developed for a local YMCA. Again, it had limited success but it was from these early beginnings that Alan went on to develop a wide range of practical, workable and successful coaching programmes, the latest having an independent evaluation by Canterbury Christ Church University.

The strategy

He started by writing programmes for children of all ages to create a sound foundation of self-esteem and confidence. We have to feel good about ourselves before we can do any personal development work. On top of this, we need an understanding of how our thoughts and feelings affect our behaviour. When we become truly aware of this, we can move on to develop our creativity and connect with our inner knowing.

This will help us to connect with our intuition which is, consciously or - for most of us - subconsciously, the driving force in our lives. Many of you might recognise this as your 'gut feeling' or instincts. Generally we ignore this in order to 'keep the peace' externally at the expense of our feeling good internally. He believes that, when we 'listen to our intuition', we are self-empowered. The earlier children learn these techniques, the more enriched and fulfilling their life will be.

Positive Parenting

It soon became obvious that, although the children benefited from the experience and it was fulfilling to help them, they still went home to the same environment. He realised that, for the programme to have maximum impact, parents needed to be involved too. This motivated him to get a job as a Parenting Tutor for Medway Council where he could deliver his Positive Parenting programme. Conventional 'parenting skills/courses' tell parents what to say and do in particular situations. His unique approach asks the parents what they want to achieve by asking powerful questions to help them unlock the answers and strategies they innately hold.

This programme has been extremely successful in helping parents from all walks of life to move forward, value their children and create more respectful family relationships. He completed a whole-family coaching programme to engage all members of the family. This work has been written up in the British Association for Counselling and

Psychotherapy, CCYP Journal. He plans to extend this approach into schools and work with educators. Alan sees these schools creating an ethos of empowerment at the heart of the community.

Playing it Forward

Alan has also written courses for delivery by other professionals - including life coaches, youth workers, teachers and child development specialists. Some additional applications have been 'Train the Trainer' and a special course for foster carers and their children. Kent County Council has incorporated this programme into their training for foster carers.

He has published his first book 'Listen to your children... and they will listen to you' to break through the communication barrier. Produced a video 'Kids are really different these days' to explain how and why parenting and educational methods of the past are no longer working for today's children. Started a charity Every Family Matters and is now extending the work world wide with the establishment of a network of trainer/coaches.

With his expertise and specialist knowledge, he is in much demand by other life coaches and he has written a course on parent coaching for inclusion on the website of Fiona Harrold 'the country's top life coach' - Daily Mail.

Alan's success is based on his passion and underwritten by his coaching philosophy:

I believe every child has limitless potential. It starts as a spark catching fire and needs to be identified, protected, nurtured, developed and respected. This spark must grow into a strong flame to survive the school system, parents under pressure and the influence of some peers.

Profile

Alan Wilson is passionate about creating personal empowerment in young people and founded Develop Your Child CIC (a social enterprise) in 2002 to channel this passion. Over the last 11 years his unique approach, using advanced coaching and emotional literacy techniques has evolved and been co-created with 1,000's of children, young people, parents and professionals working in homes, Schools and Children's Centre's.

His approach has been proven to work in the most challenging of environments, having been evidenced by an independent evaluation by Canterbury Christ Church University.

Alan has written a wide range of programmes and courses for the professionals involved in supporting families including teachers and foster carers.

He has also written 2 books, the latest being "How to be a Parent Champion and add magic to your family" and produced a leading DVD "Kids Are Really Different These Days" showing how and why we need to review our parenting and education system.

Alan has a vision to change the fabric of our society from the inside out.

Qualifications

2002   Life Coaching Academy - Coach training

2002/3 Neuro Linguistic Programming - Practitioner level

2003/4 Parent as Coach Academy (Oregon) - Advance coach training (ICF accredited)

2003/9 Parenting Tutor - Medway Adult Learning Service

2005 C&G 7307 Certificate in Teaching

2005 Principle Based Psychology - Introduction

2005 The Evolutionary Institute - Advanced coach training

2005 Advanced Certificate in Education, Stage 1

2006 The Evolutionary Institute - Train the Trainer

2007/8 Industry training inc. Safeguarding Children, Children's Workforce Development Council and Common Assessment Framework

2009/11 Continuing Personal Development and elected Chair of Bligh Children's Centre Advisory Board

2012 ILM Level 5 Performance Coaching for Leadership

2013 Performance Consultants International – Transpersonal Coach Training

2013 Family Coaching Academy awarded Training Centre status by Open College Network (OCN) the adult learning accreditation body. Also Parent Champion Level 2 and 3 courses accredited by OCN as equivalent to NVQ 2 and 3

Corporate Member of the Association for Coaching
A member of the South East Coaching and Mentoring Network
A Kent County Council External Training provider

Complementary therapy training:

Reiki I and II

Emotional Freedom Technique - Switching Children on with EFT

1963 - 1973 City of London Poly - HNC Business Studies and Degree in Marketing

Appendix I

I wanted you to see how easy a coaching approach is incorporated into everyday life - and how easy it is to do.

Coaching Lessons from the film 'The Kings Speech'

by Martin Goodyer

If the movie 'The Kings Speech' doesn't win a bucket load of Oscar's then there really is no justice. It's a great piece of film making; full of wit, charm and wisdom. The fact that it's based on a piece of documented history makes it all the more interesting and enjoyable. From my point of view as a professional coach it is much more than just a great piece of entertainment; it's a demonstration of what effective coaching can do for someone who doesn't think anyone, or anything, can help with a problem that seems insurmountable.

If you haven't seen it yet then you should, not simply because it's a really good film, but because it might just change your life: It tells the tale of Albert, Duke of York who suffered from a severe stammer, thus making it difficult for him to speak publicly. In an attempt to overcome this impediment he seeks help, eventually finding a speech therapist (a coach); someone very different from the physicians he's seen up until then.

Eventually his brother Edward takes the Throne and then promptly abdicates to be with the infamous Mrs Wallace Simpson, leaving his brother Albert to become King. All of this happens of course just as war breaks out, thus requiring the now King George (Albert being perceived as far too Germanic to use), to make a stirring radio speech to the nation and the empire.

Beautifully portrayed by actor Colin Firth, the Duke of York displays all the frustration and defeatism many coaches will instantly recognise. Having no other references than his own experience, this client cannot comprehend a life without his challenging behaviour. He has developed such certainty that 'nothing can be done' that he baulks at the idea of even trying, and becomes angry with any person having the audacity to pretend that anything could be otherwise.

His antagonistic and aggressive behaviour makes him appear bad tempered and prone to outbursts of temper and intolerance. He is however simply demonstrating that all behaviour is driven by emotion; in this case the pent up emotion of confusion and frustration. The Duke of York is portrayed as being essentially a 'nice man' but afflicted with a stammer; and this stammer is the cause of his negative emotional outbursts.

However nothing could be further from the truth. In fact the negative emotions are the true cause of the problem; they are then manifested as his speech impediment. It is the emotion causing the problem and not vice versa.

However all the advice he receives is to the contrary, and all the medical expert's efforts are to no avail. That is until he meets a coach. Speech therapist Lionel Logue knew from experience that the mechanics of the problem were one thing but its cause was another entirely. This distinction was the foundation of his future success.

'The King's Speech' and Coaching

'The King's Speech' is the best advert yet that I've seen for coaching. I don't think anyone could watch that movie and both remain unmoved or unconvinced that there exist coaches who can help people change even the most difficult issues. In this instance it's a vocal coach specialising in speech therapy; yet he makes it clear from the outset that there are two aspects to achieving the desired change: The first is the mechanical, and the second, and far more important, is that of motivation and belief. Without tackling the latter, the former is at best a sticking plaster, and at worst, a waste of time.

Lionel Logue is the real hero of the film. It is that he recognises the true potential for great change and only he who keeps the faith even when his client doubts it. Of course it's not Lionel that has to make the change. It is Albert who has to work like blazes to apply what he learns.

Lionel may be presented as a therapist but he is really a personal development coach. He established with the client a set of personal goals and then applied his craft to support the client in making them happen. Here are just some examples of how any coach might instantly recognise what Lionel was doing as a great example of coaching:

Reflection

At the heart of every coaching assignment is the need for the client to reflect both on their existing circumstances and the future. Asking the question 'what do you want, and why do you want it' may not always be phrased as bluntly, but it will always be asked.

Process

Coaching is a journey and not a training class of content. One coach can easily spot another when they pay less attention to what needs to be said and more to where what they are saying is taking them.

Transparency

A simple outcome that transforms one set of circumstances into another is the hallmark of a coaching assignment. There are no hidden agendas or unspoken alternative outcomes; just the clarity and transparency of a shared goal.

Self Exploration

When being mentored one is expected to learn, when being assisted by a physician one is expected to listen, but when being coached one is expected to explore. A coach draws from the client the 'what ifs' and the possibilities of change; and by doing so begins to form the foundations of a new and more positive belief.

Questioning

Coaches rarely make pronouncements or statements but instead will ask a question; often a very probing question. Their purpose being to draw from the client the means by which change can be achieved. A coach lacks the arrogance or the ignorance because he or she already knows they don't have the answers. Answers are the sole domain of the person to whom the questions need to be asked.

Problem avoidance

Consultants do their best to provide solutions and solve problems whereas a coach will do their best to avoid the problem all together. A coach knows that it is not necessary to always kill the dragon if all you want to do is cross the moat.

Momentum

Coaches use terms that indicate movement and progression. A coach is well aware that no problem is ever truly overcome completely, but that as long as the client continues to move away from their issue, it need not ever manifest again.

Discovery

Not only is a client encouraged to self-explore but a coach too will discover new ways to be an even better coach with every client they work with. A coach is open to such discovery and as such sets themselves apart from those who purport to already know all there is to know.

Unconscious

Knowing what to do and doing it are not always comfortable bed-fellows; a coach doesn't rely on conscious awareness but will help provide unconscious triggers. By imagining themselves in the position of the client and using their detailed knowledge of that person, a good coach will bring ways of achieving change to the surface; going where no ordinary conscious activity might go.

Actions

What makes a coaching session truly effective is the continuation of the session beyond the immediate connection between client and coach. This is achieved by the client taking agreed actions between sessions that have been designed to help keep in mind the cumulative progress made.

If you have seen the film then you will have recognised Lionel as a coach by all of the above. From his initial questions to reflect on need; clarification of the approach he was to take and the goals they might achieve; deeper than anticipated questions from the outset and a focus always on the goal; an acceptance that change might take a while and would be controlled by the pace of discovery by Albert; then latterly an awareness of the specific thinking Albert was using to get him through a sentence, and the utilization of those thoughts to achieve a result. Truly an outstanding coaching job!

Copyright 2011, Martin Goodyer a good friend and colleague

www.BusinessCorporateandExecutiveCoaching.Com

Appendix II

It is very exciting to see how a coaching approach can have such a profound impact in mental health.

Life coaching for mental health recovery: the emerging practice of recovery coaching

Rani Bora, Saija Leaning, Alison Moores & Glenn Roberts

Summary

Mental health services are increasingly expected to engage in a process of cultural change to fulfil guiding values and hopes for choice, personalisation, self-determination, social inclusion and personal recovery. It is unclear how this will be achieved. This transformational agenda also engages with an ambition for progressive change in practice across mental health professions to support people in self-care and self-management, based on a new relationship between practitioners and users of mental health services. There is little consistent guidance on the content of recovery-oriented and socially inclusive practice and what may be the new competencies and skills that would most effectively support recovery outcomes. Life coaching to support recovery for people with mental health needs is emerging as a creative possibility with considerable potential to support this ambition. This is an exploratory article which offers an overview of experience so far, suggests further routes for development and, in line with the College's Fair Deal campaign, underlines the need for evaluation.

Declaration of Interest

Both R. B. and S. L. are qualified as life coaches and are interested in coaching from both a personal and professional perspective.

Tell me and I forget. Teach me and I remember. Involve me and I learn.
Benjamin Franklin

The aspirations and hopes for future mental health services are firmly set on applying the principles of recovery and finding effective and acceptable ways of enabling people who use mental health services to be in control of their own lives (Future Vision Coalition 2009). This involves not only structural and organisational changes to create new ways of working, but new forms of practice and a remodelling of skilled helping relationships to promote self-care and self-management. The ambitions of progressive policy (Shepherd 2008) and guidance (Care Services Improvement Partnership 2008) invite us to engage in a process of cultural change across mental health and social care services and stretching into society as a whole. There are clear implications for changes in workforce, training, outcomes evaluation and the nature of interactions between practitioners and people who use services (Shepherd 2009). The big issue is clarifying future practice and how to achieve this.

There is already widespread interest and experience in 'coaching' in sport and business and the possibility has been raised that this knowledge and experience could be adapted for mental health practitioners as a wellness-focused approach to enable people to become more skilled in self-care and self-management, i.e. coaching for recovery.

The College emphasises that coaching and mentoring are beneficial for practitioners (Psychiatrists' Support Service 2008; Royal College of Psychiatrists 2008) and there is extensive experience of coaching in other fields as a route to maximise potential. This article explores the initial steps of adapting these approaches to working with people who have significant mental health needs. The cross-over involved in seeking to apply an approach associated with success and thriving in high-functioning individuals to people with significant mental health problems also emphasises the common pursuit of well-being and happiness and ties in with the concluding observation in the position paper A Common Purpose that for the first time we are considering guiding principles and practices that are of equal value to the practitioner as to the service user (Care Services Improvement Partnership 2008: p. 26).

What do we mean by 'coaching'?

Skiffington & Zeus (2003) state that contemporary coaching approaches grew out of the theories and practices of Rogerian counselling based on humanistic psychology and have philosophical roots in constructivism and existentialism. 'Coaching' can be defined as a holistic orientation to working with people, to find balance, enjoyment and meaning in their lives as well as improving performance, skills and effectiveness. The term looks back to early forms of transportation, i.e. stagecoach or rail coach and literally means to transport someone from one place to another (Starr 2008). Conventionally, a coach (e.g. a sports coach) would have a specialised area of expertise and a successful track record in their particular area. Life coaches are not expected to have expertise in the specialist fields of their clients, but are expected to have completed formal accredited training to achieve core coaching competencies (International Coach

Federation 2008) and maintain professional standards through continuous professional development.

What is the evidence in support of coaching?

Despite the popularity of coaching there has been little rigorous research into its effectiveness or outcomes. There is considerable testimony in support of improved company and individual performance, increased productivity, good staff retention and teamwork, although it is often linked to promotional materials of for-profit organisations (Coaching Clinic 2004). There is some evidence for the effectiveness of business and executive coaching, including return on investment (McGovern 2001). A randomised controlled trial looking at the effectiveness of a preventive coaching intervention for employees at risk of sickness absence because of psychosocial health complaints concluded that coaching positively affects the general well-being of employees (Duijts 2008). It follows that although coaching is an established and growing approach to enhancing performance in non-clinical populations, the lack of empirical support signals a considerable need for evaluation of effective methods, outcomes and limitations if coaching is to be adopted as a method of support for people with mental health needs (Ramsay 2005).

Life coaching in the context of recovery and long-standing mental illness

There is a broad overlap between the principles of recovery and those of life coaching (Table 1). The central tenet of recovery is an emphasis on 'personal recovery' alongside 'clinical recovery' (Shepherd 2008), which has been defined as 'a way of living a satisfying, hopeful and contributing life, even with the limitations caused by the illness' (Anthony 1993); recovery is a 'unique process, a journey, with discovery of personal resourcefulness, new meaning and purpose in one's life' (Higgins 2007).

Table 1

A comparison of core principles of life coaching and recovery-based practices

Recovery principles	Life coaching principles
Recovery is about building a meaningful and satisfying life, as defined by the people themselves, whether or not there are ongoing symptoms or problems	People are not broken; they do not need to be fixed. Coaching is about uncovering what people truly want, their core values and supporting them to be aware of their own resourcefulness
The helping relationship between clinicians and people moves away from being one of expert–patient towards mentoring, coaching or partnership on a journey of personal discovery	The coaching relationship is a partnership of equals, more than anything parental or advisory

Hope is central to recovery and can be enhanced by people discovering how they can have more active control over their lives and by seeing how others have found a way forward	People have the resources and skills to make any change they want
Recovery represents a movement away from focusing solely on pathology, illness and symptoms towards focusing on health, strengths and wellness	The power of focus – what we focus on we get
People are encouraged to develop their skills in self-care and self-management in whatever way works for them. There is no 'one size fits all'	People can generate their own solutions. An individual is ultimately responsible for the results they are generating
Recovery is about discovering and often re-discovering a sense of personal identity, separate from illness or disability	The past does not dictate the future. We need to listen to and acknowledge individual people's stories and past experiences but having done so support them to create new stories and unlock their true potential by taking action to change their lives

Finding meaning in and valuing personal experience is important, as is personal faith, for which some will draw on religious or secular spirituality	The spiritual aspect of coaching looks at who we truly are and our purpose in life

a. Adapted from Davidson (2008), Starr (2008) and Achieve Coaching & Training (2007).

Traditionally, people with mental health problems have been signposted to mental health services, which aim to diminish symptoms and disabilities, rather than towards life coaching, which seeks to develop resilience, strengths and performance. Increasingly, a new emphasis is being applied to mental health practice and services, derived from perspectives of people who have personal experience of mental health problems or use of services. This puts equal or more weight on what a person is recovering 'towards' and on the need and value of building a meaningful life and pattern of living apart from illness. This has been described as the difference between clinical recovery and personal recovery and whereas one is supported by evidence-based guidelines and treatment the other is supported by recovery coaching and support for self-management (Slade 2009a).

How does coaching differ from other approaches that promote well-being?

Skills of listening, questioning and building trusting relationships are common to therapy, counselling, mentoring and coaching, as is promoting awareness, responsibility and self-belief (Whitmore 2002). Both mentoring and coaching may make use of counselling skills, but whereas in counselling proper they are usually focused on resolving particular problems, coaching and mentoring are focused on goal or role-related achievements, from 'arriving' to 'surviving and thriving', and thus include optimising success and fulfilling potential. Similarities and differences between coaching and mentoring continue to change. The College's Occasional Paper, Mentoring and Coaching (Royal College of Psychiatrists 2008: p. 6), emphasises similarities between coaching and mentoring:

> Most models of mentoring and coaching share the same basic premise, namely that the mentee is resourceful and that the key role of the mentor/coach is to help the mentee use this untapped resourcefulness.

However, there may also be differences in the relative importance given to experience or training. Preparation for coaching is dependent on being properly trained and having learned appropriate skills to an accepted level. It is therefore quite possible for an effective coach to work with someone without any specialist knowledge of their work or situation. In mentoring, the tradition has been of a more experienced colleague supporting someone with less experience and some mentorship schemes are explicitly set up on the basis that mentors will have a number of years' experience of a similar job (Roberts 2002). Coaching tends to be for time-limited sessions, whereas mentoring is often conducted in the context of a longer-term supportive relationship.

More recent models of mentoring (e.g. Connor 2007) have placed less emphasis on the prior experience of mentors and more emphasis on training in mentoring skill, which then looks very much like coaching in a mentoring role. In practice, there may be no clear distinction and the terms are often bundled together and used interchangeably. The competing merits of qualifications over qualities would ideally be resolved by the coach or mentor having both.

Values, principles and practice

Tools

Typically, the coaching process (Fig. 1) involves the use of coaching tools (Box 1) and a conversational style of probing, listening, pausing and giving the person the space and time to reflect, being mindful of staying well-connected to the present rather than the past or future. Conflict between a person's desires and core values often results in under-performance and dissatisfaction in life (Martin 2001) and is invariably addressed through coaching. Active, intuitive listening includes skills of articulating, clarifying, using metaphor and meta-view, and acknowledging (Whitworth 2005). This and skilful, outcome-focused questioning (Box 2), accompanied by genuine curiosity, are commonly used during the coaching process. Re-framing meanings attached to events or personal experiences (O'Connor 2002) helps shift perspectives and challenges world views to support and stimulate a learning process. The GROW framework (Whitmore 2002) is one of the most commonly used coaching tools to help people focus on the solutions rather than dwell on problems (Box 3). Whitmore states that the goal of a life coach is to 'build awareness, responsibility and self-belief', which compares to the main principles underlying recovery of 'hope, agency ("control") and opportunity' (Shepherd 2009: p. 1).

I ~~DON'T~~ KNOW YOU ~~ANYMORE~~

The coaching process. Adapted from Starr 2008 and Skiffington & Zeus 2000.

Fig 1

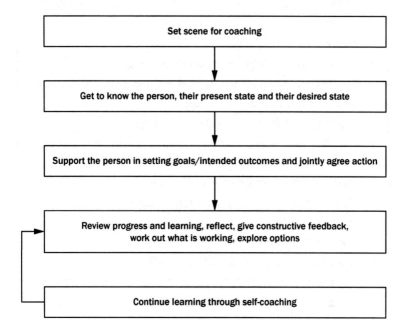

BOX 1

Examples of commonly used coaching tools/concepts

- Basic understanding of the core coaching competencies
- Application of the Wheel of Life (Mind Tools 2010) and the GROW framework (Whitmore 2002)
- Active, intuitive listening
- Skilful and outcome-focused questioning
- Identifying moving-towards and moving-away values and values that could be in conflict
- Aligning core values during goal-setting
- Awareness of basic human needs and the means used to meet them
- Re-framing meanings of experiences
- Exploring and/or jointly challenging safety behaviours or limiting beliefs
- Creating awareness

(Adapted from Asher 2004; Starr 2008)

BOX 2

Some key questions in life coaching

- What do you do differently when you are content and enjoying yourself?
- What makes you laugh or smile?
- What do you like doing? What activities would you indulge in?
- What inner qualities do you think you have that make you likeable?
- What do you value in life? What does that do for you?

- What are you doing right now to honour your core values?
- What are you putting up with that you want to change?
- What would you do if you knew you wouldn't fail?
- If you had no fear, what would you ideally do in this situation?
- If you were the coach, how would you coach yourself to win?
- If you knew the answer, what would it be?
- What would the consequences of that be for you or for others?
- Who are you becoming?
- What are you settling for?
- How are you using your gifts?
- What are you holding on to that you no longer need?
- What one thing would you change for the better?

(Adapted from Whitmore 2002; Asher 2004; Mumford 2007)

BOX 3
Planning and goal-setting by making use of the GROW framework

G = Goals
Setting clear goals (What do you want specifically?)
R = Reality
Exploring the current situation (What is happening? What action have you taken on this so far? What were the effects of that action?)
O = Options
Alternative strategies or courses of action (What are the options available for you to move forward? What else? Anything else? What are their pros and cons?)

W = Way forward

What is to be done, when, by whom and the will to do it (What will you do? Will this action meet your goal? What obstacles might you face? How can you deal with these? Rate on a 1–10 scale the degree of certainty you have that you will carry out the actions agreed. What prevents it from being a 10?)

(Adapted from Whitmore 2002; Asher 2004; Mumford 2007)

Recovery-oriented practice

Recovery coaching – the adaptation of life coaching practice and principles in support of personal recovery – is an emerging practice in wellness-oriented mental health services. Recovery coaching starts from the premise that we have common needs and aspirations and is based on what the person desires as the outcome. This includes the person making and learning from bad choices/ decisions and being honest and transparent about the limitations set by the duty of care. Borg & Kristiansen (2004) emphasised the importance of combining a high level of relationship skills such as empathy, caring, acceptance, mutual affirmation, encouragement of responsible risk-taking and a positive expectation for the future with other recovery skills as key ingredients of recovery-oriented practice. The concepts of choice and responsibility are central to coaching. Unless the person in coaching is willing to assume responsibility for his or her choices and actions, they may remain stuck in their problem state, not feeling able to act positively within their problem situation (Starr 2008).

Personal responsibility

This challenge to personal responsibility is both a difficult and pivotal shift in engaging with both coaching and recovery perspectives. The personal challenge involved has been robustly expressed by a leading activist and mental health consultant (Coleman 1999: p. 16):

> We must become confident in our own abilities to change our lives; we must give up being reliant on others doing everything for us, we need to start doing things for ourselves. We must have the confidence to give up being ill so we can start being recovered.

From a provider perspective, Watkins (2001) believes that 'People can take responsibility for themselves (though they might need encouragement to take it)' (p. 67), which underlines one of the basic principles of recovery coaching in balancing hope, aspiration, expectation and realism. However, in taking these steps Starr (2008) usefully emphasised the importance of making a clear distinction between upholding confidence that people can progressively take up personal responsibility and attributing blame to them for the situations they find themselves in.

Boyle (2003) has suggested that a core principle for coaching in mental health is the need for mental health workers to sustain confidence that people who use our services can set, own and achieve meaningful goals for themselves. But if the effectiveness of coaching is dependent on people's motivation and desire for things to change (Gash 2009), there are obvious complexities in applying coaching approaches to people with severe mental health problems.

Implications

Implications for people who use mental health services

Boyle (2003: p. 3) described the benefits of coaching in the following way:

> It [coaching] sees people in terms of their future potential, not their past performance so it offers users of mental health services the experience of achieving positive results through their own actions. Coaching in mental health complements other professional interventions by its focus on awareness, responsibility, performance and self-belief ... Doubt, fear and unhelpful thinking are addressed as they arise, as obstacles to the person's goals and only in such a way that the person develops a strategy that they are confident will lead to the achievement of the goals set. As people achieve their goals their sense of personal effectiveness, self-esteem and autonomy grow and they choose to build on their success by setting further meaningful goals.

To benefit from coaching, people need to be willing to explore what is possible, to become their own experts not only in identifying early warning signs of their illness and what works for them but also in self-management and taking personal responsibility for improving the quality of their own lives while being supported by professionals. For a coaching approach to work, both the worker and the service user must make an active contribution. These shifts of power and authority are fully consistent with the hope of a 'new relationship between users and services' identified by the Future Vision Coalition (2009: p. 26). Whatever the present capacity of people using services to engage in a coaching relationship, workers can adopt a coaching stance and set the scene for the possibility of coaching relationships to follow.

Implications for carers and family members

It is a key observation that families and other supporters of people with mental illnesses play a crucial role in their journey to recovery and often have their own needs for recovery (Watkins 2007). Enabling family members to develop coaching attitudes and skills would not only enhance their capacity to be appropriately supportive but also address their own recovery needs.

Implications for workers

Developing recovery partnerships

Slade (2009b) and others (Shepherd 2009) have asserted that a key cultural change and organisational challenge in recovery-oriented services is a shift towards helping relationships based as much as possible on partnerships. This is fully compatible with the model of role relationships in coaching, where the skills of the coach are a resource that is offered to work on the other's goals, providing choices and supporting people to develop and use self-management skills, rather than fixing the problem for them. This is also consistent with the shift of emphasis anticipated in recovery services from focusing on delivering treatment to taking a more educational stance of supporting self-care and self-management (Shepherd 2009).

BOX 4

Initiatives in the Devon Partnership NHS Trust

The Devon Partnership NHS Trust has declared a commitment to 'Putting recovery at the heart of all we do', which has led to production of a recovery guide (Devon Partnership NHS Trust 2008). This is now an accepted and widely endorsed framework describing the guiding values, principles, practices and standards of a recovery-oriented service. This includes an expectation that 'The helping relationship between clinicians and patients moves away from being expert–patient towards mentoring, coaching or partnership on a journey of personal discovery'.

This change of practice is described in the Trust's overarching policy guide Recovery Coordination (Moores 2008). It specifies that all practitioners will develop recovery coaching skills and adopt a recovery coaching stance at all levels of practice. This represents a major change process that is being led by the Executive Nurse and Trust Recovery Coordination team (led in turn by the Trust's recovery lead) through a series of master classes for clinical team leaders. This is an initial step in an ongoing process of clinical and cultural change, which will be supported by new supervision and personal development review policy, practice quality audits and key performance indicators across the Trust that monitor practitioner and team adoption of recovery-oriented practice and standards. The benefits of moving towards a coaching stance in routine practice have been described as applicable to the overall personal development of the individual people, their contribution to the team's performance and to the anticipated and intended change in work culture (Slade 2009a).

A flexible approach

Coaching can be used as either a formal coach–client approach or a
set of skills and an approach to be used in any setting (Smith 2007).
Some services emphasise that recovery coaching is a basic skill to
be developed by all staff (Box 4). Having a degree of flexibility around
the coaching style is important and with more severe problems may
become more so. The aim is to be alongside the person and work on
their goals and coach at their pace. To be able to recognise when to
be challenging or supportive, firm or compassionate is important, as
is the ability to tolerate ambiguity. It could be easier once the recovery
relationship is well established and the person is ready for change.

Understanding the individual

Those developing coaching approaches in mental health settings
also emphasise the need to understand the obstacles people face
in both engagement and progress:

> The challenge for mental health workers is to work with a
> person's own perspective of recovery, and their own goal/
> wishes ... we also need to be sensitive to the possibility that
> someone is selling themselves short, may experience internal-
> ised stigma (the notion that negative stereotypes and beliefs
> about mental illness have become part of the person them-
> selves) or feel hostile towards services on the basis of previous
> experiences. As workers helping someone on their voyage of
> recovery, we need to find a way to work with the person to
> enable him/her to remove some of the barriers to success.
> (Long 2009)

It follows that all mental health workers will need to be well versed in 'keys to engagement'. Hence Watkins (2007) has emphasised the need for the worker to seek to understand the person's phenomenological world and engage through what the individual values. Recovery coaching emphasises the need to hold hope for the people using our services, to choose to believe that they are resourceful and to have a curiosity to find out their hopes and ambitions beyond their diagnosis, stories and sufferings, reconnecting with their capabilities, strengths and resources.

Supporting workers

It is paradigmatic that a move towards recovery-oriented practices should support the well-being of the workers too (Care Services Improvement Partnership 2008: p. 26) and it is reasonable that a shift towards recovery coaching practice could have a beneficial implication for the workers' well-being, team and organisational relationships.

Implications for service systems

Coaching is an established intervention to assist organisational change (Treur 2005). Slade (2009b: p. 26) states that 'Evolving towards a recovery vision may prove impossible without fundamental transformation', which amounts to putting values into practice. It is therefore suggested that an organisation wishing to adopt a recovery orientation could beneficially adopt coaching philosophy as a support for cultural change, which will require significant investment in training for attitude, skills and qualities (Box 5; Boyle 2003). This includes incorporating recovery-supportive values into

---

BOX 5

Coaching experience of the Community Care Trust

The Community Care Trust is a third-sector organisation providing recovery services for people with mental health difficulties and a wide range of community network activities in south Devon, UK. It has 70 staff, 50 of whom are support, time and recovery (STR) workers. It works across three residential units and an open population of 400 people who become members of the service and use it on a flexible basis according to need. This service is recognised as a pioneering example of a recovery-oriented service network (Slade 2009a).

In 2006, the Trust decided to engage in a process of training and retraining for the entire staff in coaching as applied to recovery-oriented practice.

---

the relationships between the organisation and its workers, which is developed through practical tasks such as supervision, appraisals, training activities, capabilities and disciplinary procedures and which forms the leading approach to all change management. The organisation has to be clear and consistent, with its communication stating precisely why it is promoting recovery and recovery coaching so that all involved know what is asked of them and how and where to seek information and support. Finally, for a coaching culture to emerge, the contribution needs to come from leaders as role models and managers engineering operational changes and through valuing the contribution of every worker, and also through the extended network of stakeholders and other contributors.

Most of the staff have completed a locally devised recovery qualities experience training and recovery qualities coaching programme. Each participant also belongs to a coaching group which meets every other month to look at coaching in practice. These groups are led by lead coaches who have undergone advanced coaching training. The coaching groups are the main vehicle for developing practice and in this way the Community Care Trust aspires to embed the coaching principles and the recovery qualities throughout the organisation.

This fundamental reorientation of practice has brought its own challenges. Staff had to learn to understand and manage their anxieties about new ways of relating to people with new expectations of shared responsibility and co-working. As staff understood the importance of what they personally brought to the coaching relationship, it gave them confidence to experiment, learn and grow. The result was that relationships moved closer to becoming partnerships.

Further information is available from eilisrainsford@yahoo.co.uk and www.community-care-trust.co.uk

Making a start

The foundation has already been laid in terms of recognising the compatibility between the guiding values, principles and practices of recovery on the one hand and the recovery supportive potential of coaching practice and its practical applications in support of self-management, recovery-oriented care coordination, staff supervision and assessments on the other (Slade 2009a). Designing appropriate training programmes for implementation as part of continuing professional development for mental health workers would be the next step. Support for such training could emerge from National Health Service trusts (or boards in Scotland) setting up recovery education units as suggested by the Sainsbury Centre (Shepherd 2009) and there are examples of some trusts, boards and services making a start (Boxes 4 and 5; Boyle 2003). However, there is a particular need for trusts, boards and organisations setting up coaching initiatives to embed robust evaluation to support critical appraisal and ongoing learning.

Concerns and cautions

In a cautionary note, echoed by many others, Slade (2009b: p. 8) pointed out that 'It is unhelpful to put expectations on a person who is still early in their recovery (what a professional might call acutely unwell) which they cannot even begin to meet'. There is an endemic concern in mental health services that proponents of new practices underemphasise the difficulties people with severe or long-term conditions may have in being self-determining – the so called 'denial of disability'. This is one of the more frequently cited reservations in relation to adopting recovery-oriented approaches in psychiatry (Davidson 2006). A previous paper (Roberts 2008) explored the need for realistic expectations and constructive caution in the application of choice in support of recovery for people with impaired capacity who are subject to detention. However, that review and associated commentaries also upheld the proposition that there should be no 'recovery-free zones in our services', whatever the level of disorder or disability. Our traditional approaches have been generally criticised as overestimating risk and denying opportunity for discovery. Future-oriented perspectives such as that from the Future Vision Coalition (2009) and the consultation paper preparing for New Horizons (Department of Health 2009) express a clear intent to support a shift from the dominant emphasis on risk avoidance to promoting careful and creative positive risk-taking. Recovery coaching as described here would be a practice supportive of such a shift.

Challenges – personal, professional, institutional

Whitworth et al (2005) described the coaching relationship as a 'designed alliance', with the power being granted to the relationship, not the coach. In mental health settings, we face a variety of challenging situations when the perception is that the person using our service has lost his capacity to participate in such alliances or partnerships, especially when acutely unwell or detained under the Mental Health Act. The power balance then may temporarily shift towards the practitioners making decisions on behalf of the person. However, the Code of Practice (Department of Health 2008) emphasises that the guiding principles for application of the Act include being respectful of people's needs and preferences and providing opportunity to participate as much as is practicable, with the aim of promoting recovery. Much of the guidance that follows continues to emphasise taking the least control possible of someone and for as little time as is necessary. A recovery coaching stance would therefore have application even in these most difficult of circumstances when people's readiness and willingness to take on personal responsibility may be heavily compromised by past experience or present difficulties. It would also support a desirable shift from the traditional role of experts with answers to approaches that are supportive of people resuming personal responsibility and control even in the context of severe or disabling conditions.

The emerging ambition to adopt recovery coaching as a basic competency for all mental health workers creates obvious challenges for them and the possibility of their resistance or rejection of this change to traditional ways of working. Training and support for recovery coaching will need to be carefully managed so as to constructively engage the workforce. Careful evaluation of the usefulness and return on investment of such a new way of working and being would be essential.

Conclusions

Although coaching has been used in the sports and business world for many years, it is a relatively new concept in the medical and mental health world. For readers interested in learning more about life coaching we have included some sources and resources in Box 6). Recovery can be seen as reflecting 'common sense' (Amering 2008), but common sense is not necessarily common practice. If successfully supporting people to make progress in personal recovery is ever to become the common purpose of mental health services (Roberts 2007), there will need to be a development of new aspects and attitudes to practice that positively support health and well-being and engage with the radical and transformational hope of empowering people who need and use services to be maximally in control of their lives. There is a broad overlap between the guiding aims, goals, values and practices of both recovery (Devon Partnership NHS Trust 2008) and coaching and an emerging, but largely unevaluated, emphasis that applying life coaching skills in the service of mental health recovery – recovery coaching – could be a key practice for the future.

BOX 6
Sources and resources for further study and training *

Boyle D (2004) Coaching for Recovery. A Key Mental Health Skill. Pavilion Publishing.

Connor M, Pokora J (2007) Coaching and Mentoring at Work. Developing Effective Practice. Open University Press.

Martin C (2001) The Life Coaching Handbook. Everything You Need to be an Effective Life Coach. Crown House Publishing.

Mumford J (2007) Life Coaching for Dummies. A Reference for the Rest of Us. John Wiley & Sons.

Robbins A (2001) Notes from a Friend. A Quick and Simple Guide to Taking Charge of Your Life. Pocket Books.

Starr J (2008) The Coaching Manual. The Definitive Guide to the Process, Principles and Skills of Personal Coaching. Prentice Hall.

Zeus P, Skiffington S (2005) The Coaching at Work Toolkit. A Complete Guide to Technique and Practices. McGraw-Hill Australia.

Acknowledgements

We gratefully acknowledge the contribution of David Cook and other members of the Recovery and Independent Living Professional Expert Group, Devon Partnership NHS Trust.

References

Achieve Coaching & Training (2007) NLP Presuppositons. AC&T.

Amering M (2008) Recovery. Why not? Psychiatrische Praxis 35: 55–6.

Anthony WA (1993) Recovery from mental illness. The guiding vision of the mental health service systems in the 1990s. Psychosocial Rehabilitation Journal 16: 11–23.

Asher A, Hay N (2004) New Insights Pty Ltd Coach Training Program Manual 1, Version 9. New Insights.

Borg M, Kristiansen K (2004) Recovery-oriented professionals. Helping relationships in mental health services. Journal of Mental Health 13: 493–505.

Boyle D (2003) Coaching For Recovery. A Key Mental Health Skill. Pavilion Publishing.

Care Services Improvement Partnership, Royal College of Psychiatrists, Social Care Institute for Excellence (2008) A Common Purpose. Recovery in Future Mental Health Services. SCIP.

Coaching Clinic (2004) The Benefits of Coaching. Coaching Clinic (www.thecoachingclinic.com/benefits.html).

Coleman R (1999) Recovery. An Alien Concept. Handsell Press.

Connor M, Pokora J (2007) Coaching and Mentoring at Work. Developing Effective Practice. Open University Press.

Davidson L (2008) Recovery – Concepts and Application. Devon Recovery Group, CSIP, RCPsych, SCIE (http://www.centreformentalhealth.org.uk/pdfs/recovery_concepts.pdf).

Davidson L, O'Connell M, Tondora J, et al (2006) The top ten concerns about recovery encountered in mental health system transformation. Psychiatric Services 57: 640–5.

Department of Health (2008) Code of Practice. Mental Health Act 1983.
TSO (The Stationery Office).

Department of Health (2009) New Horizons: Towards a Shared Vision for Mental Health. Consultation Paper. Department of Health.

Devon Partnership NHS Trust (2008) Putting Recovery at the Heart of All We Do. What Does It Mean in practice? Devon Partnership NHS Trust (http:\\www.rcpsych.ac.uk/campaigns/fairdeal/archivedposts.aspx).

Duijts S, Kant I, Van den Brandt P, et al (2008) Effectiveness of a preventive coaching intervention for employees at risk for sickness absence due to psychosocial health complaints. Results of a randomized controlled trial. Journal of Occupational and Environmental Medicine 50: 765–77.

Foster-Turner J (2006) Coaching and Mentoring in Health and Social Care. Radcliffe.

Future Vision Coalition (2009) A Future Vision for Mental Health. Future Vision Coalition (http://www.futurevisionformentalhealth. org.uk/about.html).

Gash J (2009) Life Coaching. It's an Emerging Profession. Emap (http://www.independentlivingscotland.co.uk/page.cfm/link=158).

Higgins A, McBennett P (2007) The petals of recovery in a mental health context. British Journal of Nursing 16: 852-6.

International Coach Federation (2008) ICF Professional Coaching Core Competencies. ICF (http://www.coachfederation.org/includes/ media/docs/CoreCompEnglish.pdf).

Long C (2009) Recovery in Mental Health. Emap. (http://www.naidex. co.uk/page.cfm/link=131).

Martin C (2001) The Life Coaching Handbook. Everything You Need to be an Effective Life Coach. Crown House Publishing.

McGovern J, Lindemann M, Vergara M, et al (2001) Maximizing the impact of executive coaching. behavioral change, organizational outcomes, and return on investment. The Manchester Review 1: 1-9.

McGruder J (2001) Life experience is not a disease or Why medi-calising madness is counterproductive to recovery. In Recovery and Wellness. Models of Hope and Empowerment for People with Mental Illness (ed C Brown): 59-80. Haworth Press.

Mind Tools (2010) The Wheel of Life: Finding Balance in Your Life. Mind Tools (http://www.mindtools.com/pages/article/newHTE_93. htm).

Moores A (2008) Recovery Coordination. Policy Implementation Guide.
Devon Partnership NHS Trust (http://www.devonpartnership.nhs. uk/fileadmin/user_upload/publications/NN/Recovery_Coordina-tion_PIG.doc).

Mumford J (2007) Life Coaching for Dummies. A Reference for the Rest of Us. John Wiley & Sons.

O'Connor J (2002) NLP Workbook. A Practical Guide to Achieving the Results you Want. Thorson's Publishers.

Psychiatrists' Support Service (2008) Information Guide for Psy-chiatrists 4:
On Coaching and Mentoring. Royal College of Psychiatrists (http:// www.rcpsych.ac.uk/pdf/On%20coaching%20and%20mentoring.pdf).

Ramsay J, Kjeldsen S (2005) Can Coaching Reduce the Incidence of Stress-Related Absenteeism? ICF (http://www.coachfederation.org/ includes/docs/028-Coaching-Reduces-Stress.Ramsoy.Kjeldsen.pdf).

Roberts G, Moore B, Coles C (2002) Mentoring for newly appointed consultant psychiatrists. Psychiatric Bulletin 26: 106–9.

Roberts G, Hollins S (2007) Recovery. Our common purpose? Advances in Psychiatric Treatment 13: 397–9.

Roberts G, Dorkins E, Wooldridge J, et al (2008) Detained – what's my choice? Advances in Psychiatric Treatment 14: 172–80.

Royal College of Psychiatrists (2008) Mentoring and Coaching (Occasional Paper OP66). Royal College of Psychiatrists (http://www.rcpsych.ac.uk/files/pdfversion/OP66x.pdf).

Shepherd G, Boardman J (2009) Implementing Recovery. A New Framework for Organisational Change. Sainsbury Centre for Mental Health (http://www.scmh.org.uk/publications/implementing_recovery.aspx?ID=602).

Shepherd G, Boardman J, Slade M (2008) Making Recovery a Reality. Sainsbury Centre for Mental Health (http://www.scmh.org.uk/publications/making_recovery_a_reality.aspx?ID=578).

Shepherd G, Boardman J (2009) Implementing Recovery. A New Framework for Organisational Change. Sainsbury Centre for Mental Health (http://www.scmh.org.uk/publications/implementing_recovery.aspx?ID=602).

Skiffington S, Zeus P (2000) The Complete Guide to Coaching at Work.
McGraw-Hill Australia.

Skiffington S, Zeus P (2003) Behavioral Coaching. How to Build Sustainable Personal and Organizational Strength. McGraw-Hill Australia.

Slade M (2009a) Personal Recovery and Mental Illness. A Guide for Mental Health Professionals. Cambridge University Press.

Slade M (2009b) 100 Ways to Support Recovery. A Guide for Mental Health Professionals (Rethink Recovery Series, Vol 1). Rethink.

Smith J (2007) Therapist into Coach. Open University Press.

Starr J (2008) The Coaching Manual. The Definitive Guide to the Process, Principles and Skills of Personal Coaching. Prentice Hall.

Treur K, Van Der Sleus L (2005) The Benefits of Coaching for Employees and their Organisations. Vrije Universiteit Amsterdam (http://dare.ubvu.vu.nl/bitstream/1871/9214/1/20050013.pdf).

Watkins P (2001) Mental Health Nursing. The Art of Compassionate Care.
Butterworth Heinemann.

Watkins P (2007) Recovery. A Guide for Mental Health Practitioners. Churchill Livingstone, Elsevier.

Whitmore J (2002) Coaching for Performance. Nicholas Brealey.

Whitworth L, Kimsey-House H, Sandahl P (2005) Co-Active Coaching. New Skills for Coaching People Towards Success in Work and Life. Davies-Black Publishing.

Williams P, Davis D (2002) Therapist as Life Coach. Transforming Your Practice. WW Norton.

Multiple Choice Questions

Select the single best option for each question stem
(See the answers at the bottom of the next page)

1. Life coaching is:
a. a form of therapy
b. about advising clients
c. based in the present and the future
d. a relatively new concept in sports and the business world
e. backed by a robust evidence base to support its effectiveness.

2. Coaching and mentoring are similar in that:
a. they both bring out the best in the coachee/mentee by tapping their resourcefulness
b. both are appropriate for time-limited sessions only
c. both coaches and mentors have expertise in the specialist fields of their coachees/mentees
d. counselling skills are not important
e. both place more emphasis on the professional development of the person

3. It is true that:
a. the principles of recovery and life coaching are not similar
b. promoting awareness, responsibility and self-belief is unique to a coaching approach
c. the GROW framework is a popular tool used in therapy
d. successful coaching outcomes rely more on the coach's expertise than coachee's motivation to change
e. the recovery relationship is based as much as possible on partnerships.

4. Recovery coaching:
a. cannot take place unless a person has achieved 'clinical recovery'
b. is a stance that only 'recovery coaches' need to adopt
c. does not apply to mental health professionals
d. is an emerging practice in wellness-oriented mental health services
e. is about insisting that a person takes on responsibility for their life, thereby promoting self-management.

5. In recovery coaching:
a. the focus is on the problems rather than solutions
b. one component is identification of the person's core values and values that may be in conflict
c. a successful coaching relationship does not necessarily have to be based on a sense of openness and trust between the coach and the coachee
d. the coach has the right to disapprove of the way the coachee lives their life
e. the coach is ultimately responsible for the results the coachee is generating.

1) c 2) a 3) e 4) d 5) b

Multiple Choice Questions answers

Appendix III

'Kids are really different these days... pioneering an evolutionary world' A conference report

written by Dr Graham Taylor

November 11 2006 saw the coming together of a group of diverse yet energetically linked people from the various corners of the world. The focus of their attention was an inaugural conference sponsored by three driving forces set to challenge the way we think about and approach education and wellbeing in our complicated and apparently increasingly troubled society. 'The Energy Alliance', 'The Evolutionary Network' and 'Develop Your Child' include the exploration of energetic connections amongst their numerous 'raisons d'etre' and one of their tenets is the notion that young people from the very earliest of ages have phenomenal potential that must be unleashed in order to capitalise upon the importance of the information they hold.

Whilst the sponsors rightly deserve their acknowledgement, it must be said that the vision required to create such an event, and to draw an enthusiastic and, as it turned out, highly interactive audience was that of Alan Wilson, a man steadfastly on a path towards re-defining the ground rules within which parenting and education may be provided in the future.

The conference involved various sessions throughout the day. Mr Wilson welcomed the attendees and showed an extraordinary film of various people that profess to have unusual abilities (more of that later). He was followed by Annimac (Anni Macbeth), an Intuitive Futurist, Trend Forecaster and Life Coach, who spoke about The Secret World of Kids. Annimac had travelled from Australia specifically to be present. Multidimensional Awareness was the subject of the next session, led by Suzy Miller, an accomplished Speech and Language Pathologist and Educator from Arizona (again having journeyed specifically for the event).

Alan Wilson, an Ambassador for young people then discussed Parenting Potential before introducing Soleira Green, a Global Visionary and Evolutionist from the UK, who presented Pioneering an Evolutionary World. As you can perhaps imagine, the day was liberally topped up with questions, comments, theories and answers contributed both by the presenters and their highly interested audience.

To many people, subject matter like this is very contentious. It challenges conventional wisdom as it applies to education and teaching and health. It challenges those whose decision-making is based upon evidence, and therefore potentially opens itself to ridicule from the scientific community. It asks us to stretch outside our comfort zones in the way we think about things that have become second nature to us.

But what it also does is to ask a vital question of us all. If all those things that have become second nature to us are correct, why is it that so many things seem to be going so dreadfully wrong in our society?

To put a little more meat on the bones of this question, if we consider issues such as deteriorations in standards of education, increases in crime and unemployment, the drugs and alcohol culture and deteriorating quality standards in healthcare and hospitals, surely we must be sensible enough to consider that perhaps we don't have all the answers. Perhaps instead, if someone stands up and puts forward a theory that has even the slightest potential for benefit, we would be stupid to ignore it. Wouldn't we?

Enter Mr Wilson and his collaborators.

I'm going to cut to the chase (so to speak) and set the scene for this report. The conference explored (amongst a great many things):

- apparent flaws in our systems of education and why we should be consulting with young people to put things right

- telepathy

- parallel universes

- the facility to be 'aware', 'conscious' and 'actively communicating' within multiple dimensions at the same time

- the apparent ability to communicate with people one has never met before, located at opposite poles of the earth, in order to help each other

- certain young people that the Western World might label 'autistic' or as being on the 'autistic spectrum'

It (the conference) spoke of these young people as being particularly special. It argued that because we might find it difficult to communicate with them, this ought not to be considered their problem – rather, it is our inability. But it might just be a costly inability.

Those speakers who regularly work with such people attest to their extraordinary qualities and their capacity to help and provide incredibly valuable information.

But here comes the nub of the whole debate – in order to interact meaningfully with these people, we have to be able to communicate with them using a common language. To date, the vast majority of us seeking to have such interaction fail miserably.

Parents of people on the 'autistic spectrum' eventually tire of their failing abilities and consult with so-called authority figures for assistance – be they in the educational or medical worlds. Because such authority figures very often lack the specific qualities and abilities necessary for effective communication with these young people, they can perceive them to be problematic, challenging and abnormally overactive and demanding. Their natural response is often to seek to dampen things down by reducing the perceived over-activity.

But who is to say that the young people are experiencing abnormal activity levels? Perhaps we might instead consider that parents, educators and healthcare professionals feel the need to use these measures because of their own interpersonal inabilities with such levels of communication quality. The answer is surely not always simply to tranquillise and reduce brain activity – this may in effect amount to treating our own inadequacies. The real answer must lie in seeking to learn how to communicate much more effectively with people whose abilities are simply on a very different plane compared with our own.

We will return to this topic shortly but for the moment let's look at each of the sessions in brief.

The film recording Alan Wilson introduced was of various young people discussing how they interact and learn. It was apparent that they commonly use non-verbal communication, intuition and telepathy and that they are highly capable of multi-tasking.

They talked of the frustration the school environment can bring where the need to multi-task is ignored and the requirement is to focus exclusively on the teacher and taught materials. They spoke of the potential for and importance of mutually nurturing relationships between grandparents, parents, friends, and young people, and broached the topic of virtual relationships. They also introduced us to the concept of relationships based upon energetic exchange across dimensions. It is quite clear that of the people interviewed, some describe how they can communicate with people they have never met or spoken with (as we know it).

Annimac described how we now experience as much change in one day as our grandparents experienced in one year! The speed of change is exaggerating the differences between generations and the youngest and newest generation is now living without boundaries, as we know them. The resulting impact upon educators, parents and the business community is understandably massive, particularly for those unaware of the 'secret' world in which such young people operate.

This youngest generation knows no limits in a world in which technology dominates change. In order for us to ensure global and societal survival it is vital that we rapidly discover more about these young people, the world they live in, what we can learn from them and how our mutual interactions can influence our long-term sustainability.

Suzy Miller led an emotionally charged session in which she drew hugely and generously upon her own experiences in describing how conscious awareness exists at various levels. Whilst we are all able to know that we can taste, smell, touch, see and hear, most of us do not know that we can also appreciate energies extending beyond these five special senses.

Such multi-dimensional awareness is, she suggests, absolutely critical if we are to understand and appreciate the tremendous potential of young people. She described knowing how children are, in reality, much more than they might at first appear, having had numerous personally life-enhancing experiences through her professional interactions with them.

Using guided imagery, she sought to demonstrate that whilst it takes a particular approach in order to 'tune in' to the differing frequencies at which such young people can function, we are all capable of it if we simply make a conscious and committed decision to explore how. She introduced the wonderful term 'awesomism' as a replacement for 'autism'. The point was well taken by this knowledgeable audience.

Alan Wilson reflected upon a parenting culture based upon children being 'seen and not heard'. He argued that such an approach crippled their potential – and still does so today. The long-term effects of such approaches have contributed to our present global predicaments and he suggests that their resolution must include a dramatic re-evaluation of the way in which we parent our young people.

Such 'new parenting' must include encouragement of innate creative abilities, the learning of new levels of quality communication and much greater sharing of learning objectives. All of this of course couched in the context of loving, nurturing relationships based upon principles of equality. It is quite clear that there is a huge educational void crying out for replenishment, for the many that wish to focus their attention on improving the quality and nature of the relationships they have with their young ones.

Soleira Green drew numerous strands together in her session on the importance of 'kids, connection and consciousness' as we evolve, and how it is to our children that we must turn to be the pioneers in this respect. She described how we are now in a time in which we are capable of becoming consciously aware of all levels within ourselves, and we must begin to use our natural, innate creative abilities.

The fact is that the world is changing at a tremendous pace. It is prudent for older people to join younger people en route to the creation of the 'new world', in a spirit of co-creation. In accepting that it is to younger people that we must turn for much of the information we need to ensure our future survival and sustainability, it is the collaborative nature of such progress that will be crucial. And she argues that such collaboration must involve shifts in consciousness and an appreciation of energetic sensitivities.

Well right up front I did suggest that the subject matter was going to be somewhat contentious! It most certainly is. Much of it is of course conjecture. Most, if not all of it, is based upon anecdotal evidence (if it is based upon any evidence at all that is). Those of us with a scientific education and background appreciate that such evidence is of relatively low value.

It does appear that people with an intuitive understanding of the subject matter and the way in which it is discussed are almost speaking a different language from the rest of us. I, for one, do not comfortably speak this language. I find it difficult to accept that I am capable of multi-dimensional communication in parallel energy systems. I do not understand how I can choose to co-exchange ideas with people I've never met or spoken with before and who live on the other side of the world, using only my innate capabilities for tuning into differing energy frequencies, altered states of vibration and changing levels of consciousness.

However, in drawing towards a close, let's return to the subject of 'awesomism'. As already suggested, people labelled 'autistic' are often medicated in order to suppress what is perceived to be over or hyper-activity.

It may be that such measures are taken because of a lack of awareness of how to deal with a situation presented to people who simply know no better. It could be argued that the more appropriate solution would be to seek to learn how to communicate with these young people much more effectively. This would mean that many so-called authority figures would need to acquire new skills in order to do so.

Although I have had a predominantly scientific education, I can appreciate that to dismiss the subject matter of this inaugural conference because I do not speak the language or understand everything that was discussed, would be folly. Just because there is little hard evidence doesn't necessarily mean it is all nonsense. Evidence is generated from experimentation based upon a hypothesis, or theory. The theory need not always itself be based upon evidence.

We are faced with and must deal with various phenomena based upon fact. We are living in a world we seem intent upon destroying. We are 'enjoying' a phenomenally rapid pace of global change based upon technological advancement. We are seeing poverty reach ridiculously unacceptable levels in a societal context (not that there is such a thing as an acceptable level of poverty).

We are standing by as we create new diseases because of our exploitation of the need to satisfy human desires of an addictive nature – be they based upon foods, drugs and alcohol, gambling and finance, sex or simply greed. And yet faced with all of this, and more, we must ask ourselves another fundamental question – are we learning from our mistakes?

This was an inaugural conference. By definition it is the first of a series. At this time there is no way of knowing how many such conferences will follow. We have been introduced to a phenomenon that will gain momentum and importance from this point in time. It may eventually find its place in history as a critical new discipline for harnessing the power of relationships, and for garnering strength from the knowledge that our young people have within them.

Of one thing we can be certain. There is a small but growing band of people that have a set of skills and, dare I say it, powers, that regular folk will find difficult to appreciate and understand.

However we are told that such qualities are there to be had by all – in fact, we have them already but simply need to discover how to capitalise upon them and use them to their full potential. I, for one, would be interested in discovering more. Perhaps the second conference in the series will go some greater way towards showing us just how we can do so.

About the author, Dr Graham Taylor MBA MBBS B.Sc (Hons) MRCGP

Graham Taylor has spent more than 25 years in the Healthcare environment as a practising physician, international pharmaceutical industry executive, business consultant and coach. He has consulted for organisations large and small, and between 2003 and 2004, returned to clinical medical practice to re-skill and become familiar with the numerous and diverse changes within UK healthcare.

As well as having a busy Consultancy practice, he is presently Visiting Fellow/Associate Dean at the Bedfordshire & Hertfordshire Postgraduate Medical School, a collaborative initiative between Cranfield University and the Universities of Hertfordshire and Luton. He has also recently completed a book on Prostate Cancer written for patients and their significant others.

This article reflects the subject matter of the conference and the opinions of the conference organisers. It does not necessarily represent the views of the author whose role was to provide an accurate and independent report of the event.
© Dr Graham Taylor, December 2006

Appendix IV

Why I'm the luckiest Dad in the World

by Alan Wilson

Sometimes before we take a course of action we need to know that the voice speaking is connected to real life experience. That the person we're trusting has both come from the places we're trying to get from, and been to those places we want to get to. We want a fellow traveller who can guide us with the light of experience, and keep us entertained with tales by firelight when we're tired and low. Here's a little of my journey to date, I hope you'll invite me on your travels.

Second Beginnings

I've had a second chance to relate, love, understand and connect with those most important to me. I nearly lost it all until I realised they don't take cheques where we're all going and life happens today. Even though I was surrounded by all the material possessions and toys a successful advertising and marketing business owner could wish for, life was empty.

I'm so grateful I realised what was important... my children, people, love, and a fulfiling job.

Selfishness and Seriousness

It all started when I married for the first time late in life. We had our first born 35 years ago - Toby - an amazing life changing experience. I was serious about things then and I wanted to be the best Dad ever.

I really enjoyed getting up in the middle of the night (occasionally) to feed him and change him. What a fantastic bonding experience that was. To think that I had contributed to this wonderful small person had a very big impact on me. A couple of years later we had the fabulous Holly. I can remember being frightened because I loved them so much and I couldn't imagine what I would do if anything happened to them.

I suppose it is an easy excuse, but work took over. I became successful and enjoyed the money and trappings a growing business offered. About 4 years later I felt dizzy with the freedom and the toys I was gathering and became even more selfish, to the point I lost interest in my family; not in the children per se but other things had an impact on my time. I was looking for more... More of what, I wasn't sure but I couldn't be committed to the marriage.

Stresses, Strains and Second Chances

I saw my children every weekend for at least one day. Saying goodbye was a real wrench, I was consumed with a sense of loss and guilt every time. As they grew older, it became alternate weekends for the whole weekend. I took an interest in their progress at school, sports days and Christmas plays.

Our time together became more stressful as Toby and Holly wanted to do 'their thing' and I was torn between spending time with them and my own work and household chores. To overcome this conflict we tried an experiment. We would each take turns in choosing what we wanted to do the most - and the other two went along with it. Although I did not do everything I wanted, at least the time we spent together was quality time. We discussed our plans on the car journey or as soon as we met. This experiment was a blessing, as we could all do what we all wanted to do some of the time.

I then met someone who was to become my second wife. By now I was in my late 40's and she wanted to have children. I was enjoying my children and felt I was doing a good job (that was my perception, even though I felt so terribly guilty about leaving them) and I was open-minded about having another child.

As soon as we married the business started to get into trouble. I was determined to pull it around and fought for far too long, until in the end I was bankrupt. I lost everything.

Out of the ashes of all of that came Cassy.

I was determined to make up for the things I hadn't provided for Toby and Holly; mainly loads of quality time, being there when they came home from school and well... just being there.

The failure of the business, debt, no money and lack of self-respect put an unbelievable pressure on our marriage. It didn't last. I was heart-broken. I had to walk away from an acrimonious marriage and leave Cassy before I could make up for all the mistakes I had made with Toby and Holly. This was the worst time of my life, I felt guilty, lonely, morose - everything and everyone was against me. I had a nervous breakdown.

You may be wondering why I'm the luckiest Dad in the World?

Spain, Study and Self-Discovery

It started with the help of some counselling, some very good friends and a lovely holiday with Cassy. We went to Spain on our own for a week when she was 4 years old and she never asked for her Mum once. All of a sudden, I realised we had a special relationship and I meant something to her. I started to repair myself and to commit myself to being the best Dad on earth.

I have been through a time of self-discovery for the last few years, deciding what is really important to me. More recently I have changed my life completely. After 30-odd years in advertising and marketing I went to a life coach and said I wanted to put something back and if it had anything to do with children that would be a bonus. The coaching experience was invaluable in my self-discovery and change.

I fell in love with the idea of helping people achieve their full potential. After studying life coaching, parent coaching and Neuro Linguistic Programming, I realised the basis of any personal development is a solid foundation in self-esteem.

This was a light bulb moment as I noticed how confident Cassy was (despite the effect of the divorce, even though we tried to keep it from her) and the positive impact this had on her popularity, learning ability and sense of fulfilment. I also realised the importance a committed Dad has to the effect on their children's development.

Sharing and Social Commitment

So, wouldn't it be wonderful if every child on earth could have these positive attributes and abilities? You can be part of that magical change for your child. Coaching is all about taking that first difficult step.

I have adapted techniques from coaching, emotional literacy, NLP and from my own life experiences. I've written programmes, two books, ecourses, run workshops, produced a video to help empower children and their families and trained other coaches in our unique approach.

I absolutely love my job. Sometimes I lie awake and think back at what I've achieved. I see a group of eager, happy, smiling faces, hear some unadulterated laughter (the best sound in the whole of humanity) and recall a light bulb for a parent... it makes me feel lucky and grateful all over again - it's fantastic.

When I look back, I realise I wasn't the nicest person in the World! I was selfish, sulked when I couldn't get my own way and had an ego the size of a house. The first big lesson was that I realised I didn't love myself - that took a lot of soul searching. But an even bigger lesson by far was the realisation that I didn't love myself unconditionally. In other words I wasn't congruent within myself - now - if I can do it, you can too.

The key is finding your passion, what drives you and then living it to the full.

Stepping Forward

In creating this business, I have found an outlet for my passion of holistically developing millions of children and families all over the world - and I am on my way. I am truly living my dream and am committed to helping children and their families. Partner with me and create that change for you and your child.

I am the luckiest Dad in the World. You could be the luckiest parent in the World if you choose to be!

NB.   That doesn't mean I am a perfect Dad. Like any parent, I still have my challenges with all my children. But I believe all parents are doing the best they can with what they know and we are all work in progress. The bottom line is: the more congruent I am with myself, the better all my relationships are. I am passionate about supporting families to unleash the potential in their children.

Lightning Source UK Ltd.
Milton Keynes UK
UKOW05f2252130314

228121UK00001B/2/P